MISSIONS TO HINDUS

MISSIONS TO HINDUS

A CONTRIBUTION TO THE STUDY OF MISSIONARY METHODS

BY

LOUIS GEORGE MYLNE, M. A., D. D.

GYAN

Published by

GYAN

Gyan Publishing House
5, Ansari Road
Daryaganj, New Delhi-110002
Phone: 011-47034999, 9811692060
E-mail: books@gyanbooks.com

Distribution Network
gyanbooks.com
India, USA, Canada, UK, Australia, France

ISBN: 978-81-212-8126-3 (PB)
First Published, 1908

2nd Impression 2023

Printed at: Gyan Press, Delhi.

MISSIONS TO HINDUS
Author: LOUIS GEORGE MYLNE

MISSIONS TO HINDUS

MISSIONS TO HINDUS

A CONTRIBUTION TO THE STUDY OF MISSIONARY METHODS

BY

LOUIS GEORGE MYLNE, M.A., D.D.

RECTOR OF ALVECHURCH, WORCESTERSHIRE
BISHOP OF BOMBAY, 1876–97
SOMETIME TUTOR OF KEBLE COLLEGE, OXFORD

LONGMANS, GREEN, AND CO.
39 PATERNOSTER ROW, LONDON
NEW YORK, BOMBAY, AND CALCUTTA
1908

PREFACE

THE materials for this little book have been gathered by slow degrees, and for several different purposes. The general scheme of the whole took shape for a course of Lectures, delivered in the Diocese of Salisbury for its Higher Religious Education Society. These were repeated at Westminster, on the invitation of the late Dean Bradley, and appeared *verbatim* in the *Church Times*. I have repeatedly declined to reprint them, their extemporaneous form being too unfinished. But part of the matter embodied in them had been written for a Lecture in Manchester Cathedral, and part was expanded and rewritten for a Sermon on the Ramsden Foundation before the University of Oxford. The whole was rewritten for the *Church Quarterly Review*, and appeared there in four instalments.[1] Some rewriting, piecing, and arrangement has taken place, and some other matter has been added; in especial,

[1] For permission to reproduce as much as I pleased of the articles contributed to the *Church Quarterly Review*, I am indebted to the courtesy of Messrs. Spottiswoode and Co.

the portion on Method and Personality. This last formed the bulk of a paper read before the Brighton Church Congress in 1901.

The book now offered to the public may, therefore, whatever it is worth, be taken as embodying once for all its writer's settled convictions.

CONTENTS

PART I

PART II.—THE METHODS SPECIALLY REQUIRED FOR MEETING THE PROBLEMS OF CASTE

PART III.—RESULTS AND PROSPECTS

PART I

MISSIONS TO HINDUS

INTRODUCTION

SCOPE AND AIM OF THE BOOK—THE TREATMENT OF MISSIONS TO HINDUS AS A CONTRIBUTION TO THE STUDY OF MISSIONARY METHODS

MY aim in putting forth this book is to promote the study of Missionary Methods—a science which is still in its infancy—to assist in the compilation of a body of principles, generalised from actual experience; by the actual observance of which it has been found that the work has been promoted; by the general application of which we may be saved from that waste of power which is so sadly observable in the past.

Little has been done as yet towards even the collection of materials; though the Provincial Boards of Missions must be credited with making a beginning, with compiling *Mémoires pour servir* which will be helpful to all who come after them.

The study is as wide in its scope as that field

which is the world. My own special choice of a part of it has been regulated by the obvious reason that it was the one with which I was familiar. But the history of Indian Missions is peculiarly adapted for the purpose. The time has undoubtedly come when they can be studied systematically and scientifically. Three centuries and a half have passed over them since Xavier and the Society of Jesus made the first grand, devoted attempt to carry the Gospel to the Indies. The work of the Danish Missions, whose greatest hero was Schwartz, may be described for practical purposes as synchronous with the century before last. And in the meantime we have not been idle. The grand, enthusiastic mistakes which baffled the noblest efforts of all the earliest missionaries have been marked and turned to account. Their failures, no less than their successes, have formed the fruitful seed out of which new methods have developed. Carey, Martyn, Duff, and French did their work in Northern India on a totally different footing because Xavier and Schwartz in the South had worked and succeeded, and failed and died. We have seen many types of missions inaugurated and worked at and modified. We understand the conditions of the work, the character of the people of the country, the genius of their National Religion, the system of Caste, which is its outcome—so far as it can ever be said that Europeans understand Orientals.

And now the time has come when the subject can be studied scientifically; when the results of this hard-won experience can be ordered under general principles; when facts can be tabulated and arranged; when methods can be generalised from details; when the historical failures and successes of those who have sacrificed themselves in the cause can be traced to their radical causes; when principles can surely be laid out, on conformity to which in the past it can be shown that success has depended; when it is possible for the workers of the future to be dismissed to the task before them, no longer to struggle for themselves, through the discipline of manifold failures, towards adequate conceptions of method, but to enter on their work from the first furnished forth with the lessons of experience. My object in all that is to follow is to furnish a practical contribution towards this so desirable consummation.

For, indeed, the subject is such that its strictly scientific treatment can be turned to practical account. A marvellous unity and solidarity pervades the Hindu mind throughout its most various developments—moral, social, religious, and philosophical. And it is by remembering and allowing for this, for a homogeneity of character unequalled perhaps elsewhere, that the task of evangelising the country must be faced by all practical workers.

We are struggling to evangelise a people whose characters, in their personal development, are the outcome of social conditions more disastrously enervating and cramping than any which prevail elsewhere among a nation equally civilised. These social conditions, again, are the outcome of the national religion: they embody most faithfully, if unconsciously, the Pantheistic conceptions of the Deity, and of the relations of man with the supernatural, which constitute Hindu theology. This theology, again, in its turn, is the outcome, the absolute counterpart, of a system of ontological speculation which is ruthlessly and uncompromisingly consistent; which may be described as a spiritual Monism, carried out to its logical conclusions at any cost, moral or intellectual. Not a point in the Hindu character, on its moral or personal side, but can be shown to have its absolute counterpart in the intellectual development of the race; not a feature in the social system but can be traced to the abstract principles presupposed in their theological speculations; not one of the well-known stages, through which their religion has passed, but reflects, and that very faithfully, the metaphysical system which lies behind it.

It is obvious that a system such as this must give a splendid point of departure for the study of Missionary Methods; that its treatment can be rendered most useful, not only for missionary students who are to work themselves among Hindus, but for any one who is willing to be convinced that successful evangelisation in any part of the world must depend on the regulation of effort by a close investigation of principles.

CHAPTER I

CASTE—HINDUISM AS A SOCIAL SYSTEM

IT will be plain from the above Introduction that I am trying to bring before my readers a problem eminently practical, but one which can only be apprehended by studying in a great deal of detail, and grouping under general principles, the whole of the manifold conditions under which this world must be faced by perhaps one-sixth of its inhabitants.

The problem is virtually as follows :—

The Hindu being what he is in the actual conditions of his life—in personal character, in social surroundings, in religious convictions, in philosophical principles—what type of mission, I have to ask, what methods of missionary work, are most likely to win him to Christ, and to establish him in worthiness of discipleship if haply, by GOD'S grace, he be won?

The problem presenting itself to us under these four general aspects—moral, social, religious, and philosophical—I propose to present it to the reader by a method correspondingly inclusive. I must deal with Hindu life in its moral and its personal developments, as these are conditioned and affected by the social system of Caste, by the religious beliefs of Hinduism, and by the abstract monistic ontology which lies behind, and which accounts for, the religion; not treating any of the four as, in itself, the object of our research, but endeavouring to elucidate from each some practical apprehension of the problems which missionaries have actually to solve.

For it is on these that our thoughts are to be concentrated: all else will be subsidiary to these. We need not follow chronologically the history of any one mission, or of Indian Missions as a whole; need not sketch great characters or careers as subjects to be studied for their own sakes; need not deal with abstract principles, theological, philosophical, or religious, as the topics substantially before us.

Substantially, what I have to put forward is this—that the conditions of Hindu existence have produced a type of character, a way of looking upon life; that they entail certain great disabilities, and certain magnificent capacities; that these three sets of conditions, the social, the religious, the philosophical, are at the bottom reducible to one; that the outlook upon life which they entail, and the type of character which they produce has a corresponding unity and solidarity; and that the one grand problem before the missionary, as he approaches the Hindu world, is how to present the Gospel, and how to organise the Church, so that it shall meet, with the fullest completeness, the needs of the characters thus formed, because it solves with the most perfect success the problems of the system which has formed them.

The characters are the outcome more immediately of Hinduism as a social system, known to us under the name of Caste. Caste, the entire social system, is the outcome of the religious belief. The religious belief itself is the outcome, the necessary consequence, of a system of abstract thought, one of the most subtle, and one of the most consistent which have ever dominated men's intellects.

For attacking this fourfold problem, the most convenient point of departure will be found in the system of Caste, the huge social organisation which dominates the life of the Hindu, which regulates his every act, and which orders his every abstention.

Caste looked at simply in itself, in isolation from its proper surroundings, is essentially a social system. All the same it constitutes the religion, for every practical purpose, of hundreds of millions of people. And it moulds their personal characters to an absolutely incalculable extent. It stands as the link of connection between religion and personal character; between the religious beliefs which gave it birth and the character which, in its turn, it has produced. It accounts for the Hindu character; it is accounted for by the Hindu religion. It is more easily grasped than either—is more easily presented in the concrete than the religion out of which it has developed, can be reduced under a shorter description than the personal character it has produced. It forms the key to the entire position which missionary effort has to storm; for it is that which has riveted their religion as a chain upon the necks of the people; it is what renders the renunciation of Hinduism and the practical acceptance of Christianity an effort more exacting and more acute than aught which could ever, as I believe, be required of any of ourselves.

But, again, there is another consideration which has told perhaps most of all towards settling this sequence of subjects; namely, that Caste more than anything else accounts for the marvellous solidarity pervading the Hindu character, and constituting the genius of the nation; while it is exactly this prevailing solidarity, this homogeneity of character, which renders the subject of Hinduism, and, in particular, of Missions to Hindus, so capable of being treated scientifically.

What, then, exactly is Caste?

It is a gigantic organisation, under which all Hindu society is divided irrevocably and once for all into groups which are mutually exclusive, which are regulated solely by descent, and which are incapable of any rearrangement. Under this system every Hindu, by the fact of being born into the world as the offspring of the family from which he springs, is constituted a member for life, or for so long as he observes its regulations, of an organised, close corporation. Within this corporation there is absolutely secured to him for life every privilege, social and religious, which Hindu society can confer. Outside of this one group, he possesses not a single right except those which the law can enforce. And even his status at law is dependent to a very great extent upon the rules and customs of his caste.

And along with his standing in the caste, as the recognised condition of maintaining it, he inherits a set of regulations which orders with detailed minuteness his every action and abstention. What he may and may not eat and drink, the calling by which he is to live, the families into which he may marry, the ceremonies at the birth of his children, the adoptions by which he may replace them, the support which they will give him when he is old, their duties to his body after death—these form but a part of the prescriptions imposed on him from birth to death, as the conditions of retaining his privileges. So long as he conforms himself to them, he is certain of the necessaries of life, for Caste takes the place of any poor-law; he is sure to find marriages for his children, the one grand duty and anxiety which every Hindu has to face; he retains the two test-rights which outwardly symbolise his status—he may use the common vessels in which the caste-feasts are cooked, he will be handed the common pipe which is passed from mouth to mouth as he sits with his caste-fellows at their gatherings.

But to fail of compliance with the rules, to break them in any serious matter (beyond what is wont to be condoned by fines and degrading penances) is to forfeit them once and for all; and this means social extinction, means something worse than death. What it is I cannot fully convey, for no European can understand it. One can imagine oneself cut off at a stroke from every one who has ever been dear to him, divorced from husband or wife, a stranger to the children of his bosom, homeless, impoverished, despised, having none to recognise or to eat with him. But these, after all, are externals, and might leave the soul unashamed. What no European can picture is that this should come on him from without for the breach of a ceremonial prohibition, and that he should be conscious within that it formed but the outward embodiment of an inward, ineradicable defilement which had cankered him body and soul; that he had not only forfeited his all as far as this world is concerned, but that he, in his innermost being, was a horror of loathsome pollution to God, to man, to himself; that there had come on him, in one fell swoop, every temporal and eternal anathema by which a human being can be blasted; that there was left out of the shipwreck of his all no plank, no broken piece of the ship, by which to escape to land; nay, that there remained no friendly land to which escape might be made. A Hindu who has lost his caste has not changed his former status for a lower one with similar privileges—has not sunk from one caste to an inferior one. He is a pariah once and for ever. There remain to his nearest and dearest no means of extending him assistance. He could drag them down, he knows, into the gulf which has yawned for himself. No self-sacrifice, no effort, on their part could raise him one inch towards its edge. If he loves them, and because he loves them, he recognises as perfectly as they that it is fixed for eternity between them.

Such is Caste as a social system, upon its positive and its negative sides. Positively, it secures to each one out of the hundreds of millions of people who make up Hindu society a recognised social status, carrying with it innumerable duties, and securing inestimable privileges, in relation to one group of people. Negatively, it excuses each one from having duties, or recognising claims, towards a single human being outside that, perhaps, small group. In fact, it embodies in a system, it invests with a religious sanction, that question of the natural man which called forth from our Lord Jesus Christ the parable of the Good Samaritan; it allows, it encourages, it inculcates the perpetual selfish inquiry, "And who is my neighbour?"—that is to say, who is *not* my neighbour?—where may I fix a limitation—where may I find it fixed for me—on the further side of which no member of the human race has a right to expect at my hands one privilege, social or religious, one genial brotherly word, one thought of sympathetic regard? It intensifies the claims of society within a limited, well-defined area. But it does so at the cost of their annihilation outside of that one charmed circle. Beyond it they are simply non-existent—except so far, indeed, as it is open to lower-caste people to lay up treasures in heaven by honouring and succouring Brahmins.

Such is the system of Caste, the social embodiment of Hinduism.

But before I can make good to the reader the statement ventured above, that Caste, as a social organisation, is the natural outcome of Hinduism, regarded as a system of belief, I must display, as briefly as may be, the nature of the Hindu Creed and the system of Ontology which underlies it.

CHAPTER II

THE THEOLOGY OF HINDUISM: ITS THREE STAGES, HENOTHEISTIC, PANTHEISTIC, AND POLYTHEISTIC

CASTE has been described in the last chapter as a practical system of life, as the outward and visible embodiment of the Hindu national spirit. But I have said that this social system is the outcome, and the necessary outcome, of a religion and, again, of a philosophy—that Caste, as a rule of living, is the inevitable outcome of Hinduism regarded as a system of belief. And in order to justify this statement, I must bring out, as briefly as I may, the nature of the Hindu Creed on its purely theological side, and must exhibit, in outline at least, the system of Monistic Ontology which underlies and accounts for the Religion.

Hinduism, as we know it to-day, is a polytheistic creed, under which the popular worship is addressed to innumerable divinities. But it must always be borne in mind that this later, polytheistic, development is the outcome of earlier stages; the first, in a sense, monotheistic, the second altogether pantheistic. In the earliest stages of all, represented by the Vedic hymns, Hinduism was a worship of God, embodied in Nature, no doubt, but believed to be distinct from and above it. Sun, moon, rain, and rivers, His beneficent gifts to mankind, were adored in the Vedic hymns. But still the Giver and the gifts were not absolutely identified in this worship. He was held to be immanent in them all, but still He was known to transcend them. The pantheistic tendency was there, with all the horrible possibilities which have issued in the Polytheism of to-day. And yet in this earlier stage it was a tendency rather than a fact. God still was worshipped as God, though the immediate object addressed was something which God had made.

But a bastard Monotheism such as this was bound to make way for something worse. When once the line had been crossed which marks off the Creator from His creatures, when once any creaturely being was prayed to instead of the Creator, it became but a question of time, when a thorough-going system of Pantheism should displace this half-hearted Monotheism. And so He Who had been worshipped in Nature became actually identified with Nature in the minds of His Hindu worshippers. The Vedas, with their worship of God addressed as immanent in His works, but known to transcend them all, gave way to the Vedantic books in which the Transcendence is lost and the Immanence is all in all. You might say of the Pantheism of the Vedantas that it looks upon Nature as subsisting by the Immanence of the Deity in all things, and that it looks upon the Deity Himself as subsisting in virtue of that Immanence. As all things have their being in Him in the conceptions of a thorough-going Pantheism, so it were equally true to say that the Pantheist looks on the Deity as having His only subsistence in the One-and-All of Nature.

And so the door was set open for the hideous entry of Polytheism. For if God be identified with Nature, why, next, should Nature as a whole be alone regarded as God? Why not Nature in her every part? If the world be God, and God be the world, then why is a stone not God, and why should God not be a stone? If He be absolutely immanent in the whole, He must be equally immanent in the parts. And a part can be fashioned to resemble Him, or, in some symbolical fashion, to represent Him. If you tell an uneducated worshipper that the universe as a whole is divine, you convey very little to his mind. But show him the sculptured symbols, and tell him that "These be thy gods," and you will soon have a fervid worshipper where before you had a wondering half-believer.

And so, by a terrible Nemesis, the bastard Monotheism of the Vedas, in which God was worshipped *in* Nature, passed on through the Pantheism which succeeded, and in which He was worshipped *as*

Nature, to the third stage, the popular Polytheism, in which both God and Nature disappear from the religion of the people, though the educated may worship them still; where an innumerable troop of divinities crowd in to take their place, the embodiment of aspects of Nature, above all of human nature, and that in its least adorable qualities. For of Polytheism at least it is true that man makes God in his own image, and that the image of man himself, thus projected on the canvas of his imagination, will resemble its human creator much more in his degradation than in his glory.

There are thus three stages or phases in which we are acquainted with Hinduism—the quasi-Monotheistic stage, represented by the Vedic hymns, with their addresses to natural objects as embodiments of the Creator Who transcends them; the wholly Pantheistic phase, represented in literature by the Upanishads, in which Nature is identified with God, and God is identified with Nature; the Polytheistic stage of the Puranas, the legends of the gods and their adventures, in which stocks and stones are adored as indwelt by, nay, as being divinities—meet symbols of the beings represented, beings in whom crime and lust are held up for admiration and imitation. It is in this final stage that Hinduism must be dealt with by the missionary in approaching the uneducated classes and the women of every class.

But this religious system of Pantheism is, again, but the logical development of the consistent Monism in philosophy which conditions all Hindu thought.

I must endeavour, then, as briefly as I may, to sketch this ontological system.

CHAPTER III

THE MONISTIC ONTOLOGY OF HINDUISM, AND ITS CONNECTION WITH THE PANTHEISTIC THEOLOGY

A HINDU'S conception of existence, and therefore his ideal of thinking, is essentially what we speak of as Monism. His notion of a satisfying Ontology is the reduction of all that exists to a single, all-inclusive conception which shall leave nothing not embraced within its scope. A metaphysic, to be worthy of the name in the eyes of a Hindu thinker, must bring all things that are under a single category of thought, whether they be things on earth or things in heaven. It must bring the Infinite and the finite under a single all-embracing conception which shall abolish the distinction between them; it must get rid of any ultimate distinction between the material and the spiritual; it must reduce the One and the many to an absolute, all-inclusive unity; it must admit of no distinction between the thinker and the object of his thought—whether the thinker be God or man, and whether the object of thought be the visible universe around or the conjectured, invisible Creator, by Whom it was called into being. Monism, then, in metaphysics—the solution of the problem of existence by the final reduction of all things to a unity of being and of conception—such, on the philosophical side, is the essence of Hindu thinking.

It will be evident, I think, to the reader how close and how inevitable is the connection between the philosophy and the theology of Hinduism. They represent one tendency of thought as it issues in two manifestations. The theology and the philosophy alike are Monistic in the strictest sense. They represent, in two lines of speculation, one uncompromising intellectual determination to find, at any cost, a single, all-embracing conception, under which all objects of thought, under which all forms of being may be reduced to an absolute unity.

Does this mean, on the speculative side, that the thinker, with his intuition of personality, should be resolved into an impersonal One-and-All in which his very identity shall disappear? The sacrifice is unhesitatingly made; the personal being of man is declared to be a mundane illusion, a moment in the dream of the Unconscious.

Does it demand, on the theological side, that the Being of God the Creator shall cease to be regarded as transcendent, as distinct from the creation which He made? Then, with a like uncompromising consistency, He is blotted from the horizon of His universe as anything distinct from His creatures; He becomes a mere immanent Deity, Whose being is held to be no being apart from His mundane manifestations; Who finds consciousness, nay, Who finds positive existence, in the act of creation alone.

Does it demand, on the ontological side, that the universe, with its thousandfold variety, with the tyrannical material insistence which forces its presence upon us, be reduced to a speculative unity, indistinguishable from God and from ourselves? Then the doctrine of illusion comes in; it is *maya*, but a quasi-existence; it is a moment in the dream of the Divinity; so long as he thinks it, it is; if he ceases to think it, it is no more. "The Creator and the Destroyer are one"—so they say of the great god Shiva; he conceives of a universe, and it is; he conceives of it no more, and it is gone.

Does it demand, on the religious side, that the consciences of uneducated worshippers be assisted by symbols, or by divinities, adoration of which shall be easy? Then it takes the first workable stock, or the first suggestive stone, and it says that since all things are One, since God is everywhere and in all things, therefore God is in this stone, this stock, with its suggestiveness, is God; for God is all things that are, and all things that exist are Divine.

Does it demand, on the moral side, that but One Will be acknowledged in the universe to account for whatever comes to pass? Then the most imperious moral intuition which pervades man's thoughts about himself must give way to the demand for unification: man must cease to regard himself as a sinner, must acknowledge no Holy One sinned against. For if there is but One Will in the universe the very conception of sin is cut away, and all that man is and does is but the outcome, here and in time, of that One All-pervading Will which knows no time and no space; then man's worst deeds and his best are not his in any such sense as shall leave sin really sin. They are not only willed by God, so far as there is a God; they are the acts of God Himself, or at least of that Totality of Being in which both God and man are but unreally, impersonally immanent. Then God and man, holiness and unholiness, sin and goodness all merge in the impersonal One-and-All, which cannot be moral or immoral, which is simply and inevitably non-moral.

There is little need, I think, to point out how a system like this is opposed to the primary assumptions on which Christianity is based. A Christian can accept no philosophy which abolishes the primary distinction that marks off the finite from the Infinite, and discriminates matter from spirit. His consciousness of himself as a thinker, distinct from the objects of his thought, is to him the very primary conception which reduces the chaos of sensation to the order of realised knowledge. His conception of the manifoldness without him is the necessary correlative, it is true, to the unity which he finds within. But it is essentially as distinguished from one another, as counterparts to each other's distinctness, that he knows the One and the many.

Above all things, to him the First Cause can be no impersonal Absolute, indistinguishable from all that It has produced. To the Christian, God must be Personal, or He is not what we mean by Divine.

Philosophy, in a word, to be Christian, must retain as its fundamental assumption an unfaltering belief in personality, in that distinction of Me from Not Me, which is the ultimate basis of personality; and that both in the region of the finite, in which we subsist ourselves, and in that other realm of the Infinite, without whose distinction from the finite philosophy contradicts Christianity.

From the purely intellectual side, apart from the practical reason, there is much to be said for sheer Monism. It has its numerous votaries in Europe—both a quasi-spiritual Monism such as that which I have described under Vedantism, and a rigidly materialistic Monism, approaching nearer to the Buddhist position.

Once blur the fundamental distinction which Christianity assumes as axiomatic, between spirit and matter, Infinite and finite, Creator and creature, and it is mainly a matter of temperament, which factor of these primary antinomies be resolved into non-existence—whether Pantheism resolve the creature into being but a mode of the Creator, or Materialism resolve the Creator into a figment of creaturely imagination; whether Pantheism resolve the finite into a moment in the Being of the Infinite, or Materialism look on the Infinite as merely a high-sounding title for expressing the limitations of our thought; whether Pantheism look upon matter as being merely a background for spirit, or Materialism explain away spirit as a convenient unifying term for gathering up into a whole our permanent possibilities of sensation. In any case a consistent Monist will say that Christianity, as a system, has nothing whatever to teach him.

For his system has a rigid consistency to which the categories of the Christian are unable, intellectually, to pretend—if only because, in strict logic, to enforce the existence of the finite is, so far, to limit the Infinite, while to believe in an Infinite at all is to leave no standing for the finite.

But now I must justify my contention that Caste as a social system is the natural and inevitable outcome of the Monism of Indian metaphysics, and the Pantheism of the Hindu religion.

CHAPTER IV

THE CONNECTION OF CASTE AS A SOCIAL SYSTEM WITH THE RELIGION AND THE PHILOSOPHY OF HINDUISM

TWO points will stand out luminous, I trust, as following from the study of Caste, which I offered above, in the second chapter.

First, regarded as a code of obligations, it is essentially based upon Collectivism: it makes the group, and not the individual, the unit of its whole moral system. And, second, as the consequence of this, it obliterates once and for all the distinction, so familiar to ourselves, between moral and positive obligations. The connection of these two characteristics is obvious, I think, at a glance. Let the individual cease to be the unit; let every obligation of duty put forward its demands on our obedience under no "Categorical Imperative" of eternal force and application, based on no first principles of right which apply to all men for all time, but simply as a single item in a code prescribed to oneself by the accident of birth into a group—let this become fully effected, and it is plain that moral duty, as distinguished from positive obligation, is conclusively banished from one's horizon.

And such, in effect, is the result. To be born into an hereditary group in which thieving, and thieving alone, is recognised as one's hereditary occupation—this is no hypothetical case, but one which may be seen in the concrete—to be born into such a caste means to accept as one's rule of life that to prey upon the property of one's neighbours is as distinctly a virtue in oneself as it is a virtue in men of other castes to toil at the ancestral occupations which they, like oneself, have inherited. Between their obligations and one's own there is absolutely no moral difference, because each presents itself to the individual as the form of positive obligation which he was sent into the world to fulfil.

I was once encamped with a missionary near a village in the districts of Ahmednagar, when some people of a wandering tribe came and pitched their tents near ours. The missionary invited them to his tent, and spoke to them of the Christian religion. When they asked to be told more about it, he went through the Commandments with them. But when he came down to the eighth, they asked what they would have to do if they embraced the Sahebs' religion—"for we get our living by stealing; we have inherited this occupation, and we have no other to turn to."

Right means then, in the mouth of a Hindu, conformity to the rules of his caste; and wrong means violation of such conformity.

To bring this out by an illustration.

A caste regulation may be violated involuntarily as well as wilfully. The touch of a low-caste man who is forced up against you in a crowd, the shadow of such a man, or of any unclean beast, passing over your food as you cook it, will render you ceremonially unclean. I could offer instances more lurid, but let the following suffice. I had a friend, a colonel in the Staff Corps, by whose side, at the battle of Maiwand, a high-caste man was shot down. As he gasped in the agonies of death, and called out, half-delirious, for water, the colonel gave him water from his flask, and in the act of swallowing it he died—when the colonel overheard, to his horror, how the sepoy next in the ranks, with a gesture of shuddering hands, cried aloud, "His caste is lost!"

Far, far worse obliquities, which need not be touched on here, are the result, in the Hindu character, of this confusion of the positive with the moral, this obliteration of the moral by the positive.

Now, whence this extraordinary perversion, pervading the character of the Hindu, of a people whose intellectual advancement is as lofty as that of the Brahmins? To what in their character as a whole can we trace this obliteration of a principle so absolutely patent to ourselves?

It might be said, I admit, with much truth that

group-morality, with all that it entails, is far from peculiar to India, that it is found in every civilisation at a certain stage of development. Yes, at a certain stage of development. But therein lies the essence of the question. Why is it that we find it in India at quite another stage of development, along with a degree of advancement in other departments of life which ought to have caused it to slough off, and to make room for something more adequate? Why is it that it is adopted and sanctioned, with tremendous religious enforcements, among people so essentially civilised as the educated classes of India? Why is it that the completeness of its application is so absolutely drastic as it is?

A contrast will exhibit the *rationale.* The Jew has erred, and erred grossly, by exalting ceremonial obligations to the depression of weightier matters. But there has always remained for him a possibility of total recovery, and an immense immediate mitigation, the result of his rigid Theism. He has a code of moral obligation based deep upon the character of Jehovah; and to this he can continually recur, to save him from losing altogether his belief in the supremacy of the moral, in the comparative unimportance of the ceremonial.

Now this is exactly what is wanting in the case of the slave of Caste. So far from being modified or ameliorated by an ultimate sense of obligation owed by man to a Personal Deity, the moral system of

Caste is the outcome, the social expression of a drastic, uncompromising Pantheism.

This comes out into lurid relief in those hideous, immoral legends about the gods and their many adventures, which are the standing opprobrium of India. How is it, a Christian exclaims, that the frantic destructiveness of a Kali, the horrible lasciviousness of a Krishna, are attributed, in all sober seriousness, by the mass of their innumerable adorers, to beings held to be divine? How is it, as we are always being told, that no virtue can be too sublime to be inculcated in some Hindu book, yet no crime can be too revolting to be attributed to some Hindu god?

The explanation is simplicity itself when one has grasped the Pantheistic principle which underlies, and accounts for, the whole. God and man, to a Hindu Pantheist, are merged in, are but realisations of, the non-moral, the impersonal One-and-All which can alone be held really to exist. In the conceptions of such a believer, *to be* and *to be divine* are identical; to exist is all one with to be divine. All that is, or that seems to be, at all, is only a manifestation, an effortless, inevitable realisation of some of the infinite possibilities which lie, have ever lain, must ever lie in the womb of the impersonal Infinite. Whatever exists, then, is divine. Were it not a manifestation of the divine, then it would not be at all.

All facts, under a system like this, must impartially

be considered divine facts. Since kindness is a fact, it is divine; and since vindictiveness is equally a fact, vindictiveness too is a divine fact. Since purity exists, it is divine, is directly to be attributed to God. And since impurity, alas! exists also, it too must be set down to the Divinity. To say that aught is true of humanity is to have said that it is true of Divinity. For between the two there is no real distinction. God, Nature, individual men, you yourself, all you are and all you do, are regarded, in the outlook of Pantheism, as alike manifestations, realisations, of the one impersonal Being, which is Infinite, which is Absolute, which is all things. Apart from manifestations of the divine, nothing else has any existence. And apart from such realisation in the detail, in what we call the finite, the Divine, the Absolute, the One-and-All has none other than a negative existence. It exists because all things alike are predicable of it, and are actually to be found in it. It, He, the Divinity, the All has an existence so absolute, so universal that to predicate aught of it in detail is to limit it, to tie it down to the particular, and so to be unworthy of its Infinity. If, therefore, you speak of Divinity in the abstract as being holy, without admitting that it may equally be unholy, you are reducing yourself to the utter contradiction of limiting, by your particular predication, what you have assumed at the outset to be illimitable. Call God loving, and deny that He is vindictive, and so far forth you have limited His Infinity. Call Him pure, and deny that He is the opposite, and again you have contradicted yourself in terms. And, in the same way, everything, moral or immoral, may be predicated of some special god, if you think of the Divinity in the concrete—as alone the uneducated conceive of it.

For God, in the thought of a Hindu, is no transcendent Being, with any conceivable existence apart from His immanence in all things. By this immanence do colour and life accrue to that absolute Being which, apart from such immanence, were indifferent, were colourless, in fact were naught—pure being, all one with pure nothing. Man, Nature, God Himself are, then, to the Hindu Pantheist not merely "such stuff as dreams are made of": they are, in the ultimate analysis, but the dream of the Divine One-and-All. He dreams of a universe, and it is, so far as it can be said to exist. The dream passes, and the universe with it. God conceives of me, and I am. He ceases to conceive of me, and I vanish. I conceive of God, and, for me, He is. Nor has He any absolute existence, distinguishable from absolute nothing, except as He is thus conceived of.

No possible relation of responsibility, no divine categorical imperative can be based on this metaphysic of nothingness, which is also and essentially pure Being. There is no transcendent Divinity, to Whom the universe and man owe obedience; for He cannot be distinguished in fact from the universe, and from man, which have to pay it. Nor can they be distinguished from Him; they are but His manifestations. They have no responsibility to Him; for apart from Him they do not exist. He makes no requirements of them; for, after all, they are but Himself in some one of His possible manifestations. We can neither obey nor disobey Him in any real sense of the words; for all that we render or refuse is His own very act or abstention, realised in and through us. The very distinction itself between being and not-being, between action and abstention, between actual and possible, belongs to the half-lights-whole-shadows which make up the illusory consciousness of beings such as ourselves. They cannot be posited at all of the absolute, illimitable One—of which alone true existence can be predicated, so far as it is predicable at all.

I have dwelt with much persistence upon this, in the hope of conveying to the reader the hopeless moral tangle in which Pantheism involves its votaries, the web of realised illusions which the missionary has to clear up before he reaches the consciences of his hearers.

Mr. French, afterwards Bishop of Lahore, was addressing an audience one day in one of the bazaars at Agra on "righteousness, temperance, and judgment to come"; when one of them, a Hindu devotee, asked what was the good of it all, since, "as the dolls are made to dance in a puppet-show, so man is made to dance at the will of the Deity; so that there is neither sin nor virtue, nor joy nor sorrow; in truth it is *maya*, an empty show."

Responsibility, and free, moral choice, the turning-points of Theistic morality, are once and for all ruled out by the system embodied in Caste; much more the doctrine of grace, of a mystical divine assistance enabling the will of the creature.

We must pause for a moment over this. It is by contrast with the doctrine of grace—nay, why should we not go further?—it is by contrast with experiences of grace that one can learn in its most chilling desolation what Caste morality means. To have a pattern shown us, as in the Mount, an ideal set up for our attainment—Divine and Human at once—and then to be set forward to its attainment, equipped with a power not our own; to have the Spirit of Jesus within, enabling us to rise in our practice to some imitation of His example; to know that each effort of our will can be guided, informed, sustained by the Might of Omnipotence itself; to believe that in the ultimate result, begun here, effected hereafter, we can be raised into a region of holiness where the stirrings of the grace which is given us shall be blended with the efforts of our hearts, till obedience become absolute and spontaneous—this it is, this ineffable blessedness, this dignity, this beatitude, this triumph, which is offered to the Christian in the Gospel. To love as we know that we have been loved, to resolve every jarring antinomy between that which we owe to our neighbour and that which our neighbour owes us, until all be resolved into a harmony in which mutual love reigns supreme—this, again, is what lies before the Christian, doing all things in Christ enabling him.

Set this, the experience of Christians, side by side with the dreary abstraction, with the "void and formless Infinite," which constitutes the All of the Hindu; in which there is no God, no neighbour, distinguishable from yourself or from one another; nay, in which there is no self and no universe, but all is a dream, an illusion. What sanction—nay, what possibility—is left, whereon to build your life?

Here it is that Caste steps in. Be the system what it will ontologically, be the religion what it will in the ultimate and abstract analysis, life goes on, and it cries aloud for regulation. In this fancied existence of ours, in this Divine-human dream of a universe, there are needs, there are dependencies, there are relations. That dream of the One-and-All is self-realised not only in me, but in other dream-creatures like myself. They are around me, they affect me, they touch me; my dream at least includes their existence, their dream somehow trenches upon mine. And where there are contacts and relations, be they real or be they illusions, there needs must be some regulation to order their daily disposal. It cannot be found, it is plain, in any relation of obedience, as Christians understand the word, to a Being transcending us and ruling us. For obedience means liberty, means choice, presupposes a Ruler and a ruled; and all these are, *ex hypothesi*, excluded. Nor can God bid us love our fellow creatures as He has Himself loved us: for this presupposes a distinction between Him and us and them, which is, *vi terminorum*, ruled out.

Caste lays, then, a basis for morality in the only bed that is left for it. It abandons once and for all the very thought of the individual man as the unit of social existence, the very thought of personal liberty, as the turning-point of social relations. It takes a basis of absolute Collectivism as that whereon to build. It seizes on the root-conception which underlies so much of morality in early civilisations, and treats every human being as simply a member of a group. It leaves him no standing-ground, no choice, as a separate, responsible personality. It substitutes a corporate rule of life for any, even rudimentary, conception of personal liberty or choice. A morality of detail is still possible where a morality of principle is excluded. There may be an apotheosis of the Positive where the Moral has been depressed out of existence. And this is the essence of Caste—a morality of positive obligations, a morality of detail without principle. It takes the primitive conception of the group, and crystallises it, under the influence of Pantheism, to survive into a state of civilisation which ought ages ago to have sloughed it off. And it enforces it under the awful anathemas which I have tried to make real to my readers.

This is why Caste stands forth as the deadliest of all the opponents which the Gospel has to grapple with in India. It may form in the minds of the many no conscious embodiment in society of the Monism of Hindu metaphysics, or of the Pantheism of Hindu religion. But none the less surely or firmly—the more surely, more firmly, perhaps, for being embodied in a form purely social—does it chain the conceptions of the people to the limited, positive code embodied in, "Who is my neighbour?"

For it is absolutely consistent with itself—as much so as it is absolutely homogeneous with the religion and the philosophy which underlie it. The caste-group marks the limit of obligation, because it, and it alone, gives alike the foundation of the obligation and the sanction by which it is enforced. Your duty is owed to the caste, and you owe it a different duty from what members of other castes are called to acknowledge to them. Your duty presents itself, that is, under no categorical imperative which is binding on all men alike, with none of the awful sanction which is the outcome of eternal principles. No "Stern daughter of the Voice of God" has addressed herself, could ever address herself, to the votary and the slave of Caste. For him there can never come the day

> "When love is an unerring light,
> And joy its own security."

For him there can be no "stern Lawgiver" to wear "The Godhead's most benignant grace"; since the eternal principle of duty has for him no meaning, no existence. The sole reason, to him, for his obligations is the accident of his birth into his caste.

Nor does all this stand as anything μετέωρος—accidental, isolated in his life. It has grown, and could not but grow out of the categories, the presuppositions, from which there have developed for his race their philosophy, their religion, their character. Monism in philosophy, Pantheism in religion, Caste in society—they are absolutely linked to one another, form one homogeneous whole, of a ruthless uncompromising solidarity.

Now it is to consciences thus cramped and debauched, into lives thus enervated and depressed, that the message of the Gospel must be brought. With no morality but group obligations, positive, based on no principle; with consciences accustomed from childhood to learn from the legends of the gods that the divine is only linked with goodness as including the highest with the lowest, as being alike the fairest and the foulest which man can devise or carry out, because both, because all things, are divine—thus must Hindus approach the Gospel. Or rather—for they do not approach it with any spontaneous movement—thus the Gospel must find the Hindus when it makes its approaches to them.

And it is Caste, their social theory of practice, which embodies all the hideous affirmations, which enforces all the ghastly negations, that follow from the religion and the ontology.

The type of character produced by Caste, and the methods by which it must be dealt with, will require full separate treatment. But before going on to this treatment, it were well to sum up very briefly this account of Caste in itself—what it is as a social system, and how that social system is the natural, the inevitable outcome of the religion and the philosophy which lie behind it.

Hindu life, then, I have ventured to affirm, forms a perfectly homogeneous whole in its three great constituent elements.

In its moral and social aspects, under which it is known to us as Caste, it owns a detailed system of obligations; all of them purely positive, with no grand moral principle to polarise this amorphous conglomeration; without even a line of demarcation between moral and ceremonial precepts; with no higher binding obligation than that of traditional rules, which vary indefinitely in detail; and with no universal application outside of particular groups. As the group, with its ancestral qualifications, forms alike the unit of society and its ultimate constituent element, there is no room under the system of Caste for individual liberty on the one hand, or for universal obligations on the other. "The ultimate in either direction," of which νοῦς is made the faculty in the *Ethics*, is simply non-existent for Hindus, as forming a basis for obligation. *Thou shalt obey the rules of thy caste* forms a summary of Hindu morality—complete, without exception, without pity, without scope for any larger outlook, without allowance for any modifying circumstance; law without equity, without principle; law for law's sake; law to which obedience is everything, since the spirit, as distinguished from the letter, is neither acknowledged in fact nor regarded as possible in the abstract.

And this system of detailed sociology, so far from standing isolated, unsupported, in Hindu life as a whole, depends at every turn on an elaborate system of religion, of which it is the natural outcome. That religion, polytheistic to-day, as it was henotheistic originally, is yet in its spirit and essence pantheistic to the very core. It acknowledges no distinction between the worshipper and the object of his worship. While it presents to the unreasoning masses a multitude of individual divinities to be worshipped, and, alas! to be imitated—bodied forth in the grotesquest of idols before the eyes of undiscriminating adorers—set before them in the grossest of legends as food for prurient imaginations—to the initiated it treats of these divinities, and of their worshippers, cultured or uncultured, as being only manifestations, realisations, of an Entity, absolute, unconditioned, universal to the point of universality where pure Being is all one with pure Nothing. "That is thou, Thou art that" is the summary of the religion and the philosophy of which Caste is the social equivalent—which is to say that the ultimate initiation, the revelation which constitutes for the neophyte the final withdrawal of the veil, is the acceptance, with all that it involves, of the absolute indistinguishable identity which obtains between worshipper and Worshipped, between the soul of the individual man and the One, the Infinite Spirit which is God and Nature and All.

In this aspect the metaphysic and the religion may be regarded as one and the same. Speak of God, and the system is a theology; speak of nature, of the universe, of the All, and you are treating the same system as a philosophy. For, as Dr. Liddon so perfectly expressed it, under a consistent system of Pantheism "God is only a fine name for the Universe."

The connection between the abstract doctrines (be they regarded as philosophical or as religious) and the concrete social system (be it regarded as socia or as moral) is that the denial of personal identity, involved by the abstract doctrines, cuts the ground from under the feet of morality as, in any sense, a matter of principle, as something to be pursued for its own sake, as a universal "categorical Imperative," and leaves nothing as a basis for life but the detailed, the positive, the impersonal, as embodied in the conventions of a group.

Thus it comes that to the Christian evangelist, when he attempts the conversion of the people, there is presented, as a power of resistance, a non-Christian organisation, homogeneous, all-embracing, without breach, which pervades the whole life of the people, and which extends its tremendous power, with uncompromising consistency and solidarity, over every department of that life, from the most abstract conception of pure Being to the minutest details of conduct.

And now I have to bring before the reader what type of individual character this system has actually produced, after reigning undisturbed among Hindus during æons of their social existence.

CHAPTER V

THE TYPE OF CHARACTER PRODUCED BY CASTE, MORE ESPECIALLY IN ITS INTELLECTUAL ASPECTS

I HAVE attempted to sketch in brief outline the three grand leading elements—philosophical, social, and religious—which are so marvellously welded together into the one homogeneous whole of Hindu life and thought; the elaborately organised society subsisting under the rules and conditions summed up in the single word, Caste; the equally elaborate religion which lies behind the social system and finds in it its natural expression; the ruthlessly consistent ontology which, again, lies behind the religion and accounts for its every development. But in dealing with each of the three I have subordinated all that I had to say to the one grand object before us, the clear presentation to my readers of the actual type of men and women with whom the missionary to Hindus has to deal.

A certain type of character has been forcibly stamped upon the people by the domination, throughout many centuries, of the grinding social slavery entailed by observance of Caste. Will and intellect have been moulded under its pressure into a grovelling moral submission which has crushed the very longing for freedom; until abject acquiescence in slavery has caused that the abnegation of freedom

> "Should eat itself into the life of life,
> As saffron tingeth flesh, blood, bones, and all."

The fatalism involved in sheer Monism has done away with the sense of responsibility. Hideous sensual legends have grown up, as a filthy accretion, round the characters of a crowded Pantheon, each of whom is only an embodiment of a Pantheistic, non-moral One-and-All, and have debauched the national conscience out of any clear perception of an absolute right and wrong.

On the other hand, the social bonds which are forged by community of Caste form a wondrous binding link between all its privileged members. They feel themselves close to one another in proportion as they are narrowly shut off from having duties towards any one else. And in the narrower circle of the family the ties of affection and of blood subsist with a most pervading power. The parents so absolutely live again in the lives of their children and descendants, that the individual, whose very personal existence is rendered so doubtful to himself by the Pantheistic doctrine of illusion, is able, perhaps just for that reason, to believe that his own very being is bound up into his domestic relationships; so that he loves his own as himself—as an extension, an external realisation of his own proper personal existence, so far as he believes in it at all.

The type of character produced by all this I am to try to present as I may.

Now, in attempting to discharge such a task, I find myself confronted at the outset by one grand initial difficulty, so great as to be all but insuperable—that writer and readers are Westerns, and that the character to be presented is Oriental of the Orientals. The mutual incomprehensibility of the two it were hardly possible to overstate. To say nothing of missionary experience, it is the cross of every official who represents the English in India that the longer he lives in the country the less, in innumerable ways, does he believe that he will ever understand it: that to the last he will be irritated and disappointed to find that our motives and our principles, our most treasured theories of justice, and our most disinterested executive acts are accepted by the people whom we rule as the crotchets—inevitable, of course, and happily beneficent on the whole—of a nation whose thoughts and whose ways are a mysterious dispensation of Providence, to be endured since it cannot be amended. As a fervently imaginative child looks on at the ways of his elders, and wonders how people who might be playing spend their time in reading books or paying visits, so a Hindu surveys the British system, administrative, judicial, and financial, and marvels how it ever came about that human beings should behave so unaccountably. That in a country not inhabited by lunatics—for that, after all, is the strange part of it—there should be subjects who make the laws, and sovereigns who conform to them, thus made; that men should give precedence to women; that there should be boys who can choose their own trades, and girls who need not marry unless they like; that a coachman should chirrup to his horse when he wants him, of all things, *to go on;* that chaste women should dance with men, and yet should think it scandalous and wrong that unchaste women should be called in to stand up and do the dancing by themselves; that when a man beckons to his servant he should do it with his fingers turned upward, and that when he has done with his umbrella he should set it with its tip turned downwards; that a wife should call her husband by his name, and not speak of him modestly as "my *that*"; that it should be a crime to torture a bullock to make it draw an impossible weight, and yet be considered no harm to kill it and to feed upon its flesh—all these are but ordinary instances of the difficulties that Hindus encounter when they try to understand Europeans. And from these we may fairly infer how far we understand Hindus. In a word, from the commonest actions, at the hither end of the scale, to the ultimate, inexpressible categories which colour, nay, condition, all thought, a Hindu addresses himself to everything in exactly the opposite attitude from that which is instinctive to ourselves.

If only they would let us alone—would see how what commends itself to them is put out of court for us by the very fact that it is natural to themselves!—this perhaps would sum up very fairly the attitude of the Indian mind to all that an Englishman tries to do for him.

And this difference keeps breaking out in quarters the most unexpected. When you have been learning to think about the people as sunk in material interests, you learn that somehow and somewhere, at the back of his incomprehensible mind, an Oriental is essentially an idealist; that the hand which has clutched so fast over the coin so sedulously pursued is capable of a different clutch, in which it will close upon itself, through a lifetime of ascetic devotion, until the nails shall grow out through the back of it; that all that we have ever conceived of as endurance and force of will shrinks away abashed and belittled before what can be accomplished and endured among people whose general characteristic is abject and unashamed weakness.

I expect, then, nay invite, every reader to make allowances—to discount what I shall say by remembering that I describe the indescribable. But in so far as I am capable of presenting them, I am to try to set forth the conditions—intellectual, moral, and spiritual—under which the Hindu lives, and to depict the personal character which results from those conditions; the output, in individual men and women, of the tremendously homogeneous system which makes up caste-life as a whole.

And, first, of the intellectual assumptions which condition the outlook upon life in its most nakedly practical aspects. If a Hindu thinks at all, he thinks along the lines of a pure Monism. Or if he does not think himself, he knows that all thinking people who, to him, deserve the name, have reached Monism as the end of their thinking. And this implies an all-pervading scepticism about all the surroundings and conditions under which man's life is lived, nay, about that very existence in which we seem to ourselves to subsist; for it is all the mere apparent outcome, the spiritual self-realisation of Pure Being, which is also Pure Nothing.

I have had occasion more than once to try to bring home to young people this Hindu scepticism about life. An illustration which has served very perfectly with school-boys or intelligent children may not be entirely out of place in writing for older readers. Cut a hole in a sheet of black paper, and hold it up with a light behind it. Is that hole, through which the light comes, to be regarded as something or as nothing? It has sides and corners and a centre—a remarkable equipment for a nonentity! Yet the reason why the light comes through it is *because there is nothing there.*

The very sophistry and absurdity of the puzzle represent very fairly, I think, the outrageous juggling with thought which a system of Monism involves, the state of intellectual bewilderment produced on the ordinary intellect, the openings for scandalous evasion afforded to a weak moral sense.

Human life, in the eyes of a Hindu, is much like the hole in the paper. Regarded in itself, it is nought. It derives a seeming existence from some quite undefinable relations which it has with an Unknowable One and All. As the paper, dark in itself, invisible from the light being behind it, yet comes into relation with our sight by the fact that a rift has been made in its monotonous, non-cognisable uniformity, so the Absolute, the Unknowable, the One, the pure Being, which is also pure Nothing, displays itself, or seems to display itself—makes a kind of illusory appeal to be regarded as conditioned, as having relations—through the rift in its colourless continuity represented by man's life and thought. A something which is wholly unsubstantial, yet through which the light appears, does serve to adumbrate to us that there is, that there must be, Something greater—non-cognisable, for us non-existent, yet inevitably seeming to exist—demanded as a necessity of thought; because apart from its Unknowable Being, which we yet must envisage as real, our own little finite dream would have no existence at all. We are, or we seem to ourselves to be, just because the Self-realised, the Absolute, if it be only by a breach in its continuity, by a variant, not really existing, in its unconditioned, invariable totality, somehow causes that our dream has come about—that we have relations, if we have no self-existence.

The result of a creed such as this must be, can only be, on the purely intellectual side, a boundless, all-pervading scepticism about ever attaining to truth. Any system which can possibly be propounded as having a claim to acceptance, to the total submission of the intellect, has first to encounter the difficulty that the minds to which it is presented have been trained, or have missed all training, along the lines of a subtle agnosticism which goes down to the foundations of thought, and extends to its ultimate results.

Nor must it be supposed for a moment that it is only the educated, the thinkers, on whose life, intellectual and moral, this system takes practical effect. To begin with, an intellectual atmosphere in which thinkers alone can breathe freely yet tells on the minds of non-thinkers to a very real degree. Though theories about the One and the Many are no whit more comprehensible to the bulk of the people of India than they would be to the masses among ourselves, they yet work in the impalpable fashion in which the thoughts of other philosophers are wont to be unconsciously reproduced in the minds of their contemporaries and fellow-countrymen. "I know," said the Parisian *perruquier*, in the early days of the Encylopædia, "that I am only a wretched tradesman. But"—with an air of immense self-importance—"but I do not believe in a God any more than my neighbours do." And little as a low-caste Hindu may know of the Vedantic philosophy, he does not believe in *himself* any more than the most abstract philosopher, who believes that he believes—believes that if he really existed then he really would believe—that himself and the divine One-and-All are indistinguishably and absolutely the same.

CHAPTER VI

THE TYPE OF CHARACTER PRODUCED BY CASTE, MORE ESPECIALLY IN ITS MORAL ASPECTS

ONE moral characteristic of Hindus, most odious in the eyes of an Englishman, is accounted for, and to a great extent excused, by this same intellectual scepticism. It is proverbial among Englishmen in India that a native is incapable of truthfulness; that where the truth would serve his turn it is a lie which rises naturally to his lips. With exceptions, the charge holds good. But the vice is not to be regarded as being wholly on the moral side. It is, in at least equal proportion, a failure on the side of the understanding. A moral vice it is, because the Indian is, by nature and by history, the *φύσει δοῦλος*—the born slave—of Aristotle; and because, in consequence of this, his leading idea about a fact is that it may possibly be turned to advantage, and that, in a world of giving and taking, it is well that this advantage should be jealously retained for oneself. But it is a radical defect of the understanding; because the Hindu sees no reason why two contradictory statements should not be equally true.

And to a mind persuaded of this it certainly must appear hard that, out of the two alternatives, he should not be allowed to put forward the one which is convenient to himself; or—which comes perhaps to the same thing—the one which will please his interlocutor. It is no uncommon experience with cross-examining barristers that when they ask a native witness some simple question of fact they are met with "*jo hookoom, saheb*" :—whichever your honour pleases.

Be it remembered, again, in this connection, that history, as we understand it, hardly forms a part of Hindu literature. To strive by patient investigation to arrive at accurate facts about the past of the human race appears to the Hindu mind a most unnecessary and unintelligible piece of trouble. After all, when you have searched and have written, what can it matter to any one whether the facts, so called, of the past are stated in this way or in that?—perhaps they never happened; who knows whether you or your heroes have ever existed at all?

Thus a subtle sense of unreality, of the nothingness of life and its content, pervades, like a kind of miasma, the thought of the Hindu community. If an intellectual effort is called for; if a truth, unrealized before, makes a call on the assent of the understanding, unwelcome, perhaps bringing with it some demand for practical self-sacrifice, there is always the obvious resource that, after all, in the nature of things, there can be no reason whatever why two contradictory statements should not be equally true. Let it be proved to absolute demonstration that A is equal to B, a Hindu still puts it to himself—"What am I or what is my knowledge? What do I, what does any one else, really know of existence as such that I need exert myself intellectually, or disturb myself in practical matters, on the ground of this supposed demonstration? After all it may be equally true that A and B are entirely incommensurable."

But let the truth propounded for acceptance be one of a different order; let it lie in the plane of thought where demonstration is necessarily impossible; let it be one whose practical result is a walk by faith, not by sight; let the system propounded for acceptance carry with it, as resulting from its truth, the sacrifice of every privilege which has ever made life worth living; let it require, on the spiritual side, a new birth to all that is noble, a passionate acceptance by the heart of allegiance to a Saviour unseen—and it will be plain how only not omnipotent is the help which intellectual scepticism will lend to the shrinkings of the flesh. One can always fall back upon *maya*, on the unreality and illusoriness of all things, and so go contentedly on, untroubled by inconvenient demands. *Prapanch*, as it is called in one vernacular, the carking care of worldly interests, the insistence of the earthly and the material, the clamorous needs of the body and the pressure of its daily demands, find a perfect intellectual fulcrum in the dim, half-realized persuasion that, after all, there is nothing to be relied upon; that we know nothing, perhaps *are* nothing which can make it worth while to look higher. Meat and drink, money and clothes—these certainly at least appear real, while perhaps no higher reality has any substantial existence. Why struggle, why agonise, why deny ourselves, when the effort, or what we call such, may be only an illusion after all—when, in any case, effort or yielding are alike but a dream and a nonentity in the eyes of those who know most?

It may be only those who have leisure, who have meditated on the problem for themselves, to whom these thoughts are conscious realities. But their paralysing effects upon effort extend through society as a whole. Tell a man—let him know without telling, through the impalpable, pervading effects which thinkers produce on non-thinkers—that his life is but a bubble, a ripple on the surface of the Eternal Stream; and the inevitable conclusion must be this—that the stream will flow on just the same whether the ripple on its surface, which is oneself, have laughingly flashed in the sun with a joyous swirl of free effort, or have sullenly murmured itself away in the blackness of accidie and sloth. The unconscious, non-moral Totality, which is all that is left of a God under the sway of the Pantheistic conception, has realised itself into consciousness, all the same, whether you, its poor manifestation, have expressed it in this way or in that, as the two Eternities met in the moment of your seeming existence.

Thus far of the effect upon character of the Monistic Ontology as such. But it has to be remembered, in addition, what shape it has actually assumed in that Polytheistic religion in which it comes home to the vulgar. On that Stream of Eternal Existence there be ripples and ripples which have emerged, some human, but some superhuman. And what of those vaster manifestations, those roaring, omnipotent swirls which embody for the people, in the concrete, their idea of Divine manifestations? What character is communicated by these to the thought of what existence ought to be? What effects will this character have upon the life of actual practice, on the inward conceptions and ideals upon which all practice is based?

The gods of the Hindu Pantheon—the concrete manifestations of the One which present themselves to the Hindu mind as the typical, characteristic embodiments of all that most essentially exists—what impression must they produce of the inmost, pervading spirit which constitutes the archetype of life? The lust and the violence of man are raised in these so-called divinities to the "measure of the stature" of the ideal which underlies the Hindu religion. They are openly portrayed, on some temples, in sculptures, the very mention of which is abhorrent to Christian decency; they are habitually typified there under conventionalised symbols of shame. And the beings thus represented, whether covertly or, in many cases, openly, are all that the uneducated have to look to as embodiments of the Perfect and the Divine. In these, they are taught, there has emerged the most perfect typical expression of That which rules all, which *is* All.

As is the Stream, the One-and-All, in its most typical, essential manifestations, such, we may be sure, it will be—other, who will care that it should be?—in its everyday human embodiments, that is to say, in the national life. Men are better, thank God, than their creeds, as surely as they are worse than their creeds. Yet the late Sir Monier Williams left on record his deliberate conviction that in the case of the lowest and worst of the many Hindu creeds, the results are as bad in real life as pessimism could infer that they might be.

Such, then, are the more abstract influences brought to bear on the character of the people by the metaphysical and religious conceptions which underlie their national life. What of the social system, of the Caste which loomed so large in all that was said above?

The first and most obvious result produced by dependence upon caste, upon a system of positive obligations not welded into anything of a whole by principles of duty or of love, is incapacity for spiritual independence, for guiding the personal life by a conscience enlightened from within.

The celebrated epigram of Aristotle that a rod, not a reason, is wanted—*κολασέως δεῖτα καί οὐ λόγου*—if any one ask the question, why we ought to do right and not wrong, must obviously miss its application if the questioner have never been taught that anything could be right or could be wrong in itself, apart from convention, from a rule of enforcement or prohibition laid down for one caste-group.

The difference between the Christian conscience, with its spontaneous morality of principle, and the caste-enfeebled conscience, with its positive morality of rule, may be brought out by a familiar illustration. It closely resembles the difference between a crab and a vertebrate creature. The crab has its skeleton outside; the vertebrate—generally, at any rate, though the tortoises constitute an exception—has its softer parts outside, supported by the skeleton within. Let the crab be deprived of its shell, and you have the state of the Hindu conscience when the skeleton of caste is sloughed off. There remains no vertebrate structure, no internal framework of principle, to regulate that which lies without—a fact, we may say in passing, having to dwell on it more fully hereafter, which accounts for not a few of the scandals, so dear to the enemies of missions, among the earlier generations of Christians.

This comes out in a practical form in an intense dislike of responsibility, an incapacity for sturdy initiative. To strike out a line for oneself, be it only in the smallest matter, to be told in outline what to do, and then left to fill up the details, is almost like physical torture to many an intelligent Hindu. I once had to call upon a clerk to work a calculation in my office, including a sum in multiplication in which the multiplier was 10. Now boys in Indian schools are taught to multiply in their heads such sums as 2½ by 3¼, and they do it with the greatest facility. But then multiplying by fractions in school entails no further responsibility, in case of the sum being wrong; while to multiply by 10 in an office, where annas and rupees are in question, is a very different thing. And so this cautious clerk proceeded gravely to write down the multiplier underneath the multiplicand, took down the 0 at the right, multiplied each figure by 1, and so brought out his answer!

But, side by side with this absurdity, I must present some graver instances of how the morality of caste can affect people's real *morale*.

Famine works have figured very largely in the recent history of India. An official experienced in their working once told me that the gravest of the difficulties against which he had to contend was the total impenetrability of the minds of his Brahmin assistants to the idea that it mattered one straw whether pariahs lived or died; whether they were brought to the works to be nourished or starved to death in their villages.

Again, it came within my knowledge that a Brahmin was impeached before his caste by an injured Mahommedan husband, the sanctity of whose home he had invaded. He was condemned and excommunicated from his caste. But for what? Not for having sinned against God; not for having injured the Mahommedan, towards whom it was not to be assumed that a Hindu owed any obligation; but on the ground of ceremonial defilement—that the unhappy sharer of his sin was not a Hindu by birth. Outrageous as such a decision must appear to the consciences of Christians, it was absolutely of a piece with the system which the judges were sitting to administer. There are castes among Hindus, within which a similar sin is esteemed no sin at all, but rather a proof of devotion, if the man belong to a family in which Krishna is held to be incarnate.

CHAPTER VII

THE TYPE OF CHARACTER PRODUCED BY CASTE, MORE ESPECIALLY IN ITS SPIRITUAL ASPECTS

WHAT sense of right and wrong as absolutely constraining obligations, apart from positive enactments, can possibly be kept alive under a system whose sense of obligation is not outraged by facts like these? What room is there in characters and hearts which know no other training than the "touch not, taste not, handle not," prescribed by the rules of a caste, for development of spiritual independence, for the self-regulation by love which is the essence of Christian morality? An absolute enfeeblement of the conscience, an inability to stand alone, a total spiritual bewilderment, is apt to be the earliest result, when once the positive force, the mere morality of detail, which constitutes caste-obligation, has been displaced by Western influences, whether these be Christian or not. This has certainly followed in effect from the secular education which is all that our Government can offer compatibly with its promise of neutrality. It is too apt to prove the case among converts to the Christian Religion.

One obvious effect of it all is a total absence of shame for inconsistencies and tergiversations, an absolute unreliability when moral courage is called for to make a stand upon matters of principle. A European may lack moral backbone, may find it difficult to stand by his friends when they have to be "seen through" a difficulty; but he is ashamed of himself; he expects to be looked at askance; he feels himself contravening a code which can, and which ought to enforce itself by stinging social penalties. A Hindu has no feeling of the sort. He will profess to espouse a cause, to make himself the associate of its champions, and will go on to the critical moment proclaiming his adherence very loudly. And then, when the stand has to be made, he withdraws, he palters, he turns back, and never considers for a moment that any excuse is required of him.

People in England were scandalised and astonished when Keshab Chandar Sen, the leader of the Brahmo-samaj, the head of the reforming party, contradicted the principles of his reform by marrying his daughter as a child to the Rajah of Cooch Behar. No Anglo-Indian was surprised—what else had any one expected?

Most difficult to grasp or to convey, yet most essential to the development of our subject, is the attitude of the Hindu mind towards sinfulness and towards actual sin. We must try to follow this out along one or two different lines, since nothing is more vitally practical for the regulation of missionary methods.

Alike, then, intellectually and morally, alike from the abstract point of view, as being seen through a medium of Pantheism, and from the moral and practical point of view, as being distorted by the influence of Caste, an adequate sense of sinfulness is foreign to the genius of Hinduism. Sin and atonement, it is true, figure large in its religious phraseology, but they mean something totally different from what Christians associate with the words. They may refer to one's own misdeeds committed in previous incarnations, and only entailing on one now defilement, the very origin of which one cannot understand or remember. Or they may refer to ceremonial omissions, to breach of mere caste-obligations, with which morality has nothing to do.

How completely their Hindu signification must be foreign to Christian ideas may be seen by referring them very briefly to the leading ideas of the system, with which the reader has already been familiarised.

The haunting sense of sin, with the tragic intensity of conviction which a Christian associates with the thought, is unaccountable—inconceivable indeed —apart from a Personal Being against Whom our sins have been committed, and apart from a personal self whose choice might have been exercised otherwise. If there be heard no voice of the Lord calling to us among the trees of the garden, we do not need any device to conceal our shrinking shame. Let that once find us out, and until the Lord God clothe us, we must remain a horror to ourselves. But before we can conceive of ourselves as called, we must believe that there is One to call—One distinct from ourselves who are called. Else the answer to "Adam, where art thou?" were, "Where Thou art, there am I; for Thou and I are one and the same." And the answer to "What hast thou done?" were, "Be what I have done this or that, Thou Thyself art the doer of it in very deed; for I have no will and no power except as Thou-in-me will and act."

Thus far of the thought of sinfulness as vitiated by Pantheism in the abstract. Now of Caste as it bears on the same thought.

Let spiritual status or want of status be matter of physical descent; let one's caste and not one's character be that which classifies one for life in the eyes of God and man; let qualification for the Kingdom of Heaven be either born with one or eternally precluded one—and the very thought of merit and demerit, of spiritual acceptance or non-acceptance, must be radically different in kind from that which a Christian entertains. What one is—what one has made of oneself under the formative power of God's grace, or what, alas! one has failed to become by neglecting to co-operate with grace—this is, and must ever be, the thought to arise before a Christian when merit and demerit are in question. What one was born—what one's ancestors have been through countless previous generations—this thought, if it be not the only one, is at least the prevailing idea suggested by the same consideration to one bred up under Caste.

It is plain, then, that both Pantheism in the abstract and Caste as its concrete embodiment must dilute, even vitiate at its source, that conception of personal responsibility which issues in the sense of demerit.

Nor is this a mere prejudiced inference from Christian thought on the subject. It was laid down in so many words by the Swami Vivekananda, the exponent of abstract Vedantism who represented it at the "Parliament of Religions." He treated it as totally absurd that man should regard himself as a sinner; since he constitutes the perfect expression of the life of the one supreme Being:[1] "Ye *divinities* upon earth, sinners! it is a sin to call a man a sinner. It is a standing libel upon human nature." And it was said in the *Brahma Vedin*,[2] "that man is eternally pure and perfect in his real self"; and, "that the distinction of right and wrong are mere appear-

[1] Quoted from Slater's *The Higher Hinduism and Christian Thought.*

[2] The organ of Neo-Pantheism in India.

ances, which will vanish as soon as the dream of life is expelled."

Nor is it but an inference, *a priori*, that it holds good in actual practice, as the moral outcome of Caste. It is displayed in the spiritual self-sufficiency of the pampered, idolised Brahmin, accustomed to believe from his birth that the world exists but for him; that it is equally the duty and the privilege of people of other castes to minister to his every necessity; that insolence of bearing on his part is only the natural expression of innate, hereditary superiority.[1]

It is in some ways even more natural in the man of an inferior caste, who has his self-respect to gain. For, to him, to be a Hindu at all, though he be not a high-caste man, is to possess a connatural sanctity, as compared with the rest of the world, which the sense of unholiness would contradict. And yet, being unclean ceremonially to men of higher castes, he needs the more to bolster himself up by refusing to admit any sinfulness which is not innate in him physically.

One must indeed have lived among Hindus to appreciate the spiritual revolution, the *bouleversement* of religious prepossessions, represented by the words

[1] Brahmin schoolboys are taught in their manuals that, in addressing a low-caste man in Marathi, they ought to use the expletive *aré*, which is expressive of contemptuous compellation, not *aho*, which betokens respect.

of the Baptist, when he warned the Jews of his day that their claim to be children of Abraham would not stand them in stead before God; that religion and natural parentage were for the future to be divorced from one another; that personal holiness, in fact, was a moral, not a physical matter.

Yet the distinction is absolutely vital, if a true sense of sin is to be developed—how vital, we may easily remind ourselves by remembering the disastrous results which follow, for morality and religion, when the doctrine of original sin, as held by orthodox Christians, is grossly exaggerated or distorted. To insist upon inbred sinfulness as an inheritance entailed upon the race, and to forget the saving clause, how it constitutes, in actual practice, a natural downward trend—how, in its essence, it is no mere status, no mere imputation to the children of sins committed by their fathers—even this exaggeration and disproportion in stating a truth of the Gospel results in a blunted moral sense, in a distorted view of the Atonement, in making the restoration of man a merely forensic substitution, a matter of vicarious righteousness, not of personal and spiritual renewal.

But let holiness and unholiness alike be regarded as matter of caste-heritage; let such sense of sinfulness as there is be associated with the belief in metempsychosis, be only the present working out of misdeeds committed—and forgotten—in innumerable previous incarnations, and it is plain that the consciousness of sinfulness, as a Christian understands the words, must be simply non-existent.

This moral and practical element, this preclusion of a real sense of sinfulness, works in, one cannot doubt, with the underlying philosophical assumptions upon which I have insisted so fully, to form a constituent element in the weird fascination of Pantheism; an element more intelligible perhaps to the mind of an ordinary Englishman than its attractiveness when regarded in the abstract. Give up my personal identity, regard myself as an impersonal manifestation of the Unconscious, the Unconditioned! Put thus, the Monistic hypothesis may seem to ourselves to be unthinkable, too absurd to need any refutation. But offer it on the spiritual side; make it a refuge for a conscience half awakened, not yet sufficiently in earnest to throw itself, crushed with self-abasement, into the arms of a forgiving Creator; do away with the consciousness of guilt without calling for the pain, the humiliation, entailed by acknowledging it to oneself; let it appeal to that instinct of self-righteousness which, alas! is so much more connatural than the genuine sense of sin—and it needs no words, I think, to exhibit its terrible fascination.

It supplies a perfect armour of self-complacency to those who have been brought up in it from childhood, who have not drunk in from the first, as a constituent element in religion, the thought of being sinners by disposition, of being in essential opposition to the Holiness of a Personal God.

Such, then, in briefest outline, are a few of the characteristics developed in the Hindu people by the system in which they have been brought up; such the *damnosa hæreditas* entailed on them by æons of Caste—the character equally homogeneous with the system under which it has developed. First, a searching intellectual scepticism about everything which presents itself to be believed; a scepticism originating, it is true, in an abstract system of Monism, but lending itself all too readily to practical dislike of responsibility, to acquiescence in established conditions, apart from troublesome scruples as to whether they are defensible or not; a scepticism displaying itself most markedly in total indifference to truthfulness about matters of everyday life.

Next, a general deficiency of *stamina* pervading the whole moral being; an indifference to right and wrong, born and bred of a system of morality which turns upon caste-obligation as its only possible fulcrum; with no reliance on principle, no principles on which to rely; backed by no categorical imperative, but varying quite indefinitely with the conventions of different castes.

Lastly, all the inevitable enfeeblement which comes to conscience and will, where there is no distinguishing line between moral and positive obligation, between physical and spiritual status, between ceremonial and moral purity; a feebleness fairly represented by the difference between the vertebrate creature, with its internal skeleton of bone, and the pulpy, invertebrate crustacean, with its external skeleton of shell.

PART II

THE METHODS SPECIALLY REQUIRED FOR MEETING THE PROBLEMS OF CASTE

CHAPTER I

OF THE IMPORTANCE OF METHOD, AS SUCH, IN THE LIGHT OF EXPERIENCE AND OF SCRIPTURE

THE problems presented by our subject have already been brought before the reader under two great leading aspects—the larger, more general, more abstract, in the chapters on Hinduism as a system; the narrower, more personal, more concrete, in those on its outcome in character.

The attempts at a solution of those problems, the varying degrees of their success, and the principles whose observance or neglect may be held to account for the variations, have now to be brought before his notice.

If my treatment of the problems, as such, in the abstract and the concrete alike, has answered at all to my intentions, one thing must be abundantly plain—the tremendous homogeneity which pervades all Hindu life, the extraordinarily complete correspondence between the practical results of the system and the principles on which it is founded. The solidarity of its principles between themselves, from whatever side they may be viewed, ontological, theological, or social, is supported by the effectiveness of Caste for enforcing them in the lives of individuals. Caste brings the individual Hindu under the yoke of his national religion with a ruthlessness and a thorough-going completeness which cannot be equalled elsewhere, not even in Judaism itself.

I must repeat once more, for the sake of emphasis, the principle which underlies the whole system—consciously thought out by the few, unconsciously assimilated by the many. For it is this single principle, embodied in a collective morality with its conscience resident in the group and not in individual souls, which results in a theoretical denial of responsibility, freedom, nay, personality, and which issues in individual lives deprived of all colour and joyousness. The absolute, indistinguishable unity of all that exists or can exist; the identity of the One with the many, of God, the Infinite, the Absolute, with the world, in so far as it exists; the all-sufficiency, the all-inclusiveness of the Absolute, the nothingness, the non-existence of the conditioned; the delusiveness of finite consciousness, as distinguished in any degree from the self-contemplation of the Infinite; the identity of subject and object in the ultimate analysis of thought; the indistinguishableness of Being and of nothingness, if once the terms be comprehended—this forms the single, ultimate category of Hindu thought in the abstract.

This forms the all-pervading assumption of Hindu theology in its completeness, the ruling principle of Caste as the Hindu social system, the desolating negation of personality which drains from Hindu lives the very sap of freedom and self-respect.

It is with this as its ultimate principle that there has come into existence in India that type of life and character, that general outlook on the world, that set of prevailing conditions, intellectual, moral, and social, which every missionary must face when he offers the Gospel to Hindus.

The methods and principles of work demanded by these conditions, the degree to which these principles have been grasped or neglected by missionaries, from Xavier's time to our own, the dependence of failure or success on their apprehension or misapprehension —these, treated historically and biographically, will occupy the next two chapters. The principles which I shall try to lay down have all been arrived at inductively from the missionary experience of the past, and from the missionary endeavours of the present. Metaphysical as are some of the conditions, the methods recommended for meeting them have not been thought out as abstractions: they are the fruit of the actual experience of many an earnest worker. For the ultimate and permanent results of work, however devoted, have depended entirely or chiefly on the degree to which the methods of working have conformed to the conditions of the country;

on the way in which certain great principles have been apprehended, adopted, carried out, or have been missed, set aside, neglected, by missionaries, individually and collectively.

THE INTRINSIC IMPORTANCE OF METHOD, AS PROVED BY EXPERIENCE AND FROM SCRIPTURE

But before I set out upon the task of laying down some principles of Method, on the observance of which in the past the success of the work has depended; whose study will form, as I believe, a condition of progress in the future, I must set down, by way of preliminary, the reasons why Method, as such, seems to me to call for study.

And first, of Method in general, as possibly the most important condition on which success depends —the most important relatively at least, the most important for the Church to consider, if it is not actually the most potent in the workings of God as we see them.

It is plain that in the course of His Providence, working out His age-long designs, God has used two human factors as the instruments through which He has wrought. System and Personality, Character and Principles, Men and Methods, whichever pair of words we may adopt—it is certain that success in the Mission-field has depended on these two factors;

that each is of paramount importance; that on the full combination of the two the highest success has depended; that either apart from the other can produce but limited results.

Personality, Character, Men—this factor is, of course, the most striking; its study is so eminently fascinating; its results are so brilliant and so palpable, that it tends to be ever to the fore, to eclipse its more commonplace congener in attracting the attention of the world.

In the early days of a mission, under the guidance of a great pioneer, it may almost appear, I admit, as though the one condition of success, all-sufficient on the human side, were simply the force of personality. By the power of a dominating character, by the all-but irresistible influence which he wields over ordinary men, the work of God goes forward. The sway of will over will, the touch of heart with heart, the quickening of intellect by intellect brings hundreds or thousands of souls into captivity to the Gospel of Christ. Then comes the inevitable break. A Schwartz is called to his rest, after nigh half a century of work, in the midst of the people whom he loved. A Martyn passes away, alone amid the wilds of Persia; his feeble, hectic body worn out, after seven years' toil, by the fiery activity of the spirit. A Caldwell, after keeping his Jubilee, retires to a home in the hills, to spend his remaining days in prayer for his children in Christ. And then the question must be asked, What remains as the κτῆμα ἐς ἀεὶ, the permanent possession of the Church? Will the work expire with the worker? or will it prove that he has laid a foundation on which lesser men than himself may build up the Kingdom of God? In a word, have System and Method re-enforced Personality and Character? If so, then the work will go on with the unfaltering pulse of a machine; though ability of the ordinary type has to step into the room of genius; though the everyday earnestness of the Church has succeeded to the fiery enthusiasm which seemed to come straight from above.

When, therefore, we compare the two forces as regards their relative importance, we must say that they stand side by side, alike indispensable to the Church; Personality for each new departure, System for continuity and permanence; Force of Character in the great Pioneers, Method in the men who succeed them. Yet even in the Founders themselves it has proved that enthusiasm and genius have depended on the humbler gifts of Method, and System, and grasp of Principle, for securing continuity afterwards.

But which, we must ask again, is the factor which the Church can secure—Genius or System, Enthusiasm or Method? Towards which must our efforts be directed? For the absence or deficiency of which may we be called upon to humble ourselves hereafter? Our part is to systematise our experience, to provide for the Church of the future a body of well-defined principles. And then, when the Heaven-sent genius is created in the Providence of God, he will find lying ready to his hand the essential conditions and means for handing on what his character shall produce.

But generalities do not go far in enforcing a thesis such as this: I must go into rather more detail; anticipating here, for a moment, by a short biographical illustration, a subject to be treated hereafter in a good deal more fulness of detail.

In the southerly regions of India, the earliest worker for God was Xavier, the Jesuit priest, who landed in 1541 and died in 1552, having spent a large part of the interval in work in the farther East. The next great worker there was Schwartz, the Lutheran minister, who laboured without interruption over much of Southern India from 1750 to 1798. A quarter of a century afterwards the Anglican Church stepped in, and took over from Schwartz's successors a considerable portion of the field. Of our own great workers there, I have selected Robert Caldwell for comparison with the two pioneers. He kept his Jubilee in India in 1888, and died there three years later.

The story of the men and their work affords three typical instances of all that I desire to put forward. Xavier, with his splendid personality, is the type of Method run mad, of Creeds and ordinances and formularies relied upon unintelligently and mechanically. Schwartz, most lovable, most winning, with a character strong as steel, and a heart as tender as a woman's, had hardly a method at all. Caldwell, with grand ability, was, I think, much less of a genius than either of his great predecessors. But along with his lovingness and his powers, he had a splendid conception of Method—an orderly balanced conception, as against its neglect by the Lutheran and its over-exaltation by the Jesuit.

What, in brief, did they severally effect? The result of Xavier's work was—I say it with sorrowful conviction—to add to the castes which he found another and a Christian caste, unintelligent, unprogressive, mechanical in its notions of observance, sadly low in its standards of conduct; content to be Christian itself, after the Jesuit conception of Christianity, untroubled by even a thought about the duty of spreading the faith; so that to-day, after three centuries and a half, the bringing of India to Christ is just as far off as before for anything that they have effected.

When Schwartz was called to his rest his work expired along with him. After a quarter of a century of declension our Church stepped into the field, and took over a portion of his territories from the hands of his disorganised successors. It is not too much to say that from whole great tracts of country Christianity had simply disappeared, and the people had reverted to heathenism; while in others a remnant remained, who hardly knew why they were Christians.

Bishop Caldwell's work to-day is as strong and as progressive as ever. He gave it a backbone of System. He knew what System could do, and where its work must stop. He realised not only what he aimed at, but how it might best be secured. And, hardly less important, he knew what to leave unattempted; knew how far afield he could go in search of disciples for Christ; how far, when disciples were made, their hearts could be moulded by man, and where man's efforts must cease, and the rest must be left to God.

This of course must be borne in mind—that Xavier and Schwartz were pioneers, and that Caldwell entered into their labours; while many of the early mistakes were the inevitable purchase-money of experience. But whatever may have caused the mistakes, the results were such as I have indicated.

So much, then, of Method in general; with a short biographical illustration of how it bears specially on India.

All this I hope to develop in writing of Xavier and Schwartz.

Now a word about the higher authority on which I base my every statement about Method and its paramount importance.

Of all the Missionaries of the Church, the grandest,

in point of personality, was undoubtedly the Apostle St. Paul. In the earlier stages of his preaching, his only resource for his work was the native force of his character: he starts without a notion of Method. When he and St. Barnabas set out, supernaturally called to their work, sent forth with the laying-on of hands, they went straight to the home of St. Barnabas, an island in the Eastern Mediterranean, offering no special coign of vantage for reaching other countries, not marked by one single characteristic in its people, its surroundings or its circumstances, to make its conversion to Christ a starting-point for a great campaign. When Cyprus has been duly gone through, they naturally make for the mainland. But not for any part of the mainland which offered remarkable advantages. And the rest of this Missionary Journey is made among cities in Asia Minor, increasingly distant from the sea, and from the centres of civilisation, among people increasingly uncivilised; until at last they find themselves in a city whose only speech is Lycaonian, and whose only inference from a miracle is that the eloquent little man must be Hermes, and—we may suppose—the bigger and more dignified, the very Zeus himself.

The beginnings of the next great Journey are characterised by a like want of method. For very obvious reasons, St. Paul, on his first setting forth, devotes himself to visiting the converts brought in on his former tour—except those in the island of

Cyprus, who might well be left to Barnabas, and who would certainly take Barnabas' part when they found that dissensions had arisen.

But after visiting his scattered converts, St. Paul still means to go on plunging deeper and deeper into Asia, getting farther at every step from the shores of the Mediterranean—that is to say from the one grand centre, round which the shock of nationalities had evolved all civilisation. He had never, so far as we can see, asked the very obvious question, whether having but one life to spend, he was spending it to the greatest advantage; whether he might not employ it better by attacking the world at its centre; whether even conversions by the thousand in distant provinces in Asia would effect as much in the long run as evangelising people by tens at important centres of influence. A soul won for Christ in Galatia was a soul redeemed, no doubt. But there things began and ended as far as Greece and Italy were concerned—as far as any place was concerned whose position, whose language, whose commerce, whose advance in civilisation gave promise of its serving as a centre, as a future point of departure. Lystra was a city, no doubt, but not "a city set on an hill," in the social sense of the words. It could influence barbarians in its neighbourhood: it could never be a centre of light which might radiate with the multifold visibility to be looked for at Ephesus or at Rome.

One great, convincing experience was to come to St. Paul later on, which would serve, with its disastrous shock, to convince him of the falsity of his method—the great Galatian Apostasy. But this lay undescried in the future, and, meanwhile, time was passing, and the powers of his strenuous life were being daily and hourly used up; while nothing as yet was being done for the dominant cities of the world.

Then came a Divine Intervention—the only one in the Acts which apparently referred to mere detail; which did not portend, and that obviously, a total alteration of principle in the working to be looked for in the Church. The Mission of Philip to the Eunuch, the sending of St. Peter to Cornelius, the call of Barnabas and Saul, each and all formed points of departure in the one grand chain of events which broke down the exclusiveness of Judaism, and opened the Church to the Gentiles.

But now the prohibition of the Spirit, in whatever form conveyed, laid, apparently, a simple embargo on a single field of labour, a field which differed in no way from many already occupied: they are "hindered by the Spirit of Jesus from preaching the Gospel in Asia." Let Bithynia, then, be tried, is the first response of St. Paul—no change whatever in his methods, but only in the details of his route. The same mysterious hindrance intervenes a second time. And so—he hardly knows why, so far as appears from the narrative—he finds himself on the shores of the Ægean. He is called to Macedonia by a vision. Philippi—"the first city in those parts," the nearest to the landing-place, the most obvious—and "a colony," full of Roman settlers—solves the problem for him at once. The whole feel of things is so different, when once he is at work near the seaboard, and in touch with civilisation, that his lesson is learnt on the spot. Never more in the narrative of the Acts do we find that one day is spent among isolated, uncivilised tribes. His life is laid out to the best profit. He has learnt to be "*δόκιμος τραπεζίτης*," a solvent banker, investing the talent of his Master in that soundest, that most lucrative of transactions, the formation of centres of influence, where every soul that he gained could become a power for Christ in virtue of its culture, of its influence, of its special, civilised opportunities. Corinth, unrivalled geographically, Ephesus, pre-eminent in heathendom, Rome as his ultimate objective, take the place of Iconium and Lystra as the scene of his remaining labours.

What plainer lesson could we have on the importance assigned to Method in the Counsels of the Spirit of God?

CHAPTER II

OF THE TWO DISTINCT TYPES UNDER WHICH ALL MISSIONS FALL, IN WHATEVER AGE OR COUNTRY—THE DIFFUSED, AND THE CONCENTRATED MISSION

THE importance of Method, as such, the impossibility of dispensing with its aid, how powerful and how devoted soever be the character and personality of the missionary, has now been placed before the reader.

I have next to bring to his notice the two great primary types, under which all Missions to the heathen seem naturally and inevitably to fall—the Diffused, and the Concentrated Mission; the Mission whose immediate aim is active aggression upon Heathenism, wherever and whenever it can be reached; and the Mission whose present objective is to be found in forming, at a centre, a body of indigenous Christians, through the power of whose consecrated lives the mass of the heathen around are, in time, to be leavened with the Gospel.

Each type is essential to Christendom if the heathen world is to be won, and each finds its prototype in the Acts. It is the wisdom of the Church, in every country, to weigh the value of each in relation to the needs of that country, and to the temperament and the circumstances of its people.

Each, I say, has its prototype in the Acts. A cursory glance at the Book might make us say that Apostolic Example was all for the diffused type of Mission—that to grapple with Judaism and Heathenism, whenever and wherever they could be reached, was the original method of evangelising. A more careful study, as I believe, will lead to a different conclusion. If there be a book in the world which bears witness to the power and to the value of the concentrated type of Mission, that book is the Acts of the Apostles.

The first great waves of conversion, sweeping thousands of souls within the Net, were each of them the immediate result, not of any aggressive endeavour on the part of the Apostles and brethren, but simply of the innate energy at work in the new-born Church by the power of the Pentecostal Spirit. The extraordinary manifestations which characterised the birth of the Church attracted the attention of the people. Devout and earnest Jews, come up to worship at Jerusalem, were some of them simply astonished by phenomena of a spiritual nature so different from their previous experiences: while others found cause of grave scandal from seeing, as they supposed, a number of disciples of Christ drunk with wine at nine in the morning. St. Peter was constrained to explanation, to earnest protest and self-defence. Thus originated the grand first address which converted three thousand souls. The inherent energy of the Spirit, displaying itself in those who had received it, attracted attention first: Conviction followed on explanation. But the initiative came from non-Christians; from without, and not from within. The Church began her own life, and its power elicited inquiry, with its inevitable result in conversions.

The next great rush into the Church came about in much the same way. The life of the Community went on in quiet, unobtrusive devotion. Prayer and teaching and miracles and Eucharists went on from day to day, uniting the disciples among themselves into a compact and organised body, sustained by the Ordinances of its Head. It asserted itself before the world, not so much by aggressive endeavour as simply by the resistless fascination of an ordered life of love.

Then one day that life broke out, as such life must inevitably do, into a notable act of charity towards one without the pale. It was for no evangelistic purpose, as far as we can make out, that the Apostles were entering the Temple. They were going to take part in its worship; only differing from the body of the congregation by the inner conviction of their hearts, that they were in actual possession of the things which illuminated souls had descried as foreshadowed by the Temple. But such a conviction as this did its work on one of the crowd. The request of the cripple for alms was what brought him in contact with the Apostles, but St. Peter had only to look at him to see that he had the rudiments of faith, was morally capable of being healed.

Whence, then, had the faith come to him, and how was it elicited now? The "favour with all the people," which the life of the Church called out, had produced in him, as it would seem, some conviction that there was in these men a power above that of this world. Then personal contact with one of them precipitates the process of conviction. The two men are thrown together in an act of ordinary intercourse; the spiritual circle is completed—the Christ-life in Peter at one pole, the faith of the cripple at the other. And the result, again, is inevitable. The Life within the Church must out; the need around must declare itself, elicited simply by the contact. Then astonishment and inquiry again—the power which is in these men is not simply a spiritual something, too refined for daily needs, incommunicable to physical nature. What are they? Let us crowd to find out. And so again comes the need for self-defence—not now against suspicions of drunkenness, but, this time, on the opposite side; against being taken for originators, where they were but transmitters, of power. The position demands explanation: admiration and adoration and gratitude must be turned in the proper direction, to the Saviour and not to the disciples. Explanation, information, and admonition come out as the inevitable resultant; although there had been, to begin with, but an outburst of the spiritual life which the Church was living within herself.

From that day the Concentrated Mission begins to expand into the Aggressive. Prohibition produces disobedience, and disobedience is visited with persecution. And, then, as a matter of course, there followed renewed activity and renewed diffusion of influence. With the Ordination of Stephen, still more with his speedy martyrdom, and with the general persecution which follows, aggressive evangelisation becomes the order of the day.

But the original Mission of all is found, I repeat it again, to have been of the concentrated type. From it the diffused type originated—as of course it will do in every case when concentration has done its work.

For, indeed, in everyday life the difference between the two types is one of immediate method, and not of ultimate aim. How large soever be the field over which a mission is working, it aims, in the ultimate result, at establishing a Christian Church, in which all the fruits of the Spirit shall be seen in their fullest development. How rigid soever the concentration by which, in the other type of mission, the area of work is confined, it aims at nothing less, in the long run, than the complete subjugation of the country to the power of the Incarnate Redeemer.

But as regards their plans of working in the actual India of to-day, there is a contrast, marked and thorough-going, between Diffused and Concentrated Missions. The head-quarters are treated in the one case as merely a base for operations, a starting-point from which to set out upon tours of evangelisation, a resting-place to which to return when powers are in need of recruiting, or when the rains forbid itineration. In the other case, the work at head-quarters is the principal care of the missionary —might be said, for all practical purposes, to constitute his vocation and his mission. In fact, the term head-quarters is almost, in this case, a misnomer. For to call one place the head-quarters is to imply that there are others attached to it; that it is a centre, and has, therefore, a circumference. Whereas, in actual fact, the work, for a very long time, is ended and rounded off where it begins.

It consists, not in missionary travels, undertaken to sow the good seed over the largest surface which can be reached, but in work carried on in one place, commencing, if God make it possible, with a nucleus of children or young people; in other cases consisting at first in winning a few adult converts. And then, having made its commencement, having secured its tiny nucleus, it goes on with its work within itself:

it concentrates all its endeavours on tending and caring for and building up a centre of Christian life; from which, if God bless the endeavour, there may radiate to the neighbouring country some power of spirit and example, attracting the attention of many to what God has done for a few.

It is true that, almost from the first, the mission which aims at expansion must have a strong element of concentration, if it is ever to answer its purpose; and that the mission which aims at concentration will have, almost from the first, some element of outward expansion, just because it is answering its purpose. But the aim in the two cases is different. The point at which each of the methods takes on, quite definitely and intentionally, some features which are proper to the other, comes later, at a variable interval according to circumstances and success.

In the case of the itinerant mission, the evangelist, with but a home at head-quarters, sets out on his missionary journeys to bring at least the proclamation of the Gospel before as many as he can reach with prudence; to offer its saving truths to as many as his voice can reach; to sweep as many souls into his net as it will hold without risk of breaking.

For here comes the critical point, here the test of this system of diffusion, here the place where the methods overlap. Here the advocate and the agent alike of the attempt to reach the greatest number have to pause, and to acknowledge to themselves that the other, the method of concentration, asserts an imperious claim to be, at any rate, the necessary complement of their own less concentrated endeavours. To have brought people into the Church is to have pledged the honour of Christendom to their training in the principles of the Gospel. The degree and the method of the training—how far they can be left to themselves, to develop, unaided by man, in sheer and solitary dependence on the grace and presence of the Spirit—this depends, to an indefinite degree, on national and individual character, on the circumstances, the temperament, the idiosyncrasies of the nascent Christian community.

And therefore there must come a time in the career of the most fervid evangelist, the most triumphant pioneer of the Gospel, at which he must pause in his labours, must ask whether his children in Christ can be left to depend upon themselves; whether there are at each centre of Christianity fit men to be teachers of their brethren. After following the method of St. Paul in forming churches here and there, can he adopt his next resource of laying hands upon some of the converts, and ordaining them as ministers to the rest? Having founded and organised a Church with an indigenous apostolic ministry, can he leave it to stand by itself, only visiting it occasionally for a time, and communicating with it constantly by letter?

Needs must that in every case a point will be

reached at some time, after which pure Christian common sense will forbid him to penetrate farther into regions where he fain would be at work; will throw him back on "confirming the churches" in the regions already overrun — in a word, when the Diffused type of Mission must take on the characteristics of the Concentrated; when building up will become the primary need; when opportunities of evangelisation will be unhesitatingly, if reluctantly, waved aside. Unless the *personnel* of the mission is recruited with ever-fresh workers, to follow out by pastoral care the efforts of the missionary pioneer, he must find himself reduced, after a time, to, at any rate, a partial abandonment of his distant preaching tours. Through his staff, if not by himself, the work of building up must go forward. And under the circumstances of most modern missions it seems almost a practical certainty that periods must constantly recur when the need for building up will be supreme. Then there must grow up at head-quarters a nucleus of pastoral work, a body of Christians, old and young, whose more perfect instruction in the Faith, or whose training for being workers themselves, will become the first care of the missionaries.

What, then, of the outlying districts, and of the isolated Christians to be found there? Have their numbers been allowed so to multiply as to render it impossible to reach them compatibly with the work in the compound? Or have those been regulated so wisely that the circumference need not be neglected while the power at the centre is intensified? Have depth and sincerity and reality been sufficiently insisted on as conditions? or has a surface acquaintance with truth been accepted as sufficient qualification before a catechumen was baptised? Has quality been placed before quantity? Has there been the slightest tendency to think of statistics for Reports, where the well-being of the nascent Church should alone have been considered and secured? Above all, what about the native teachers, or the recently-ordained native clergy? Has sufficient discernment been exercised before the laying-on of hands? Or has the Bishop been blindly determined that an indigenous ministry there should be? And has he persuaded himself, or been over-persuaded by others, that fitness existed where it did not?

SUPPLEMENT TO CHAPTER II

A CONCRETE EXAMPLE OF THE CONCENTRATED MISSION—THE COWLEY-WANTAGE MISSION AT POONA

I SHALL not be suspected, I trust, of puffing my own special work, if I try, before leaving this subject, to make it plainer by a concrete illustration. The Mission in the city of Poona, which I was privileged to launch on its way, has been worked, ever since its inception, on the lines of concentrated work.

Since Poona was visited by the plague in 1896-7 its name has become painfully familiar to many whom its ancient fame had failed to interest in its history. It was once the most important place in what is now the Bombay Presidency; being the seat of the Maratha Government, which superseded that of the Moguls, and was in turn superseded by our own. It is still, in the eyes of Hindus, the centre of Western India; its importance as a focus of Brahminism making up for its smallness of size—it has one hundred thousand inhabitants, as against eight times that number in Bombay, whilst its trade is almost *nil*. To Europeans it derives its importance from being the seat of the Presidential Government during the months from June to October, and the head-quarters of the Bombay Army Corps all the year round.

Before Bishop Douglas's episcopate—1869-75—no Mission belonging to our Church had ever worked in this place, with its pressing claims on English Christians. When Bishop Douglas elaborated a scheme for covering the Bombay Deccan with a chain of Mission stations, under the care of the S.P.G., his plan included Poona, as the central station of three; to shake hands with Kolhapur on one side and with Ahmednagar on the other.

The scheme was statesmanlike and sound, had there been means for giving it effect. As a fact, when Bishop Douglas died there were but two ordained men at work in all the three stations put together. One was at Kolhapur and one at Ahmednagar—if one even of these two was not on sick-leave in England at the time of the Bishop's decease—and Poona was being worked by native catechists, with such supervision only as could be given by a hard-worked chaplain, unacquainted with the vernacular of the district. A great accession of converts in the Ahmednagar districts, during the famine of 1876–7, made it doubly out of the question that the spiritual needs of Poona should be overtaken by the S.P.G. Indeed, from that time down to the present the resources of the Society have been strained to maintain the Ahmednagar Mission in a condition to grapple with its work. Most happily, just at this juncture the private liberality of friends enabled Bishop Douglas' successor to open a Mission at Poona. And, by a providential coincidence, the very house that was wanted for the purpose was in the market far below its value. Panch Howds, as the house is called—*Anglice*, "Five Cisterns"—stands just at the edge of the city; sufficiently disengaged to be free from insanitary conditions, at any rate of an aggravated kind, and yet sufficiently in touch to make an admirable centre for work. And other desirable properties, embarrassed, or otherwise purchasable, lay on one or two sides of the compound, to be acquired as funds should come in. One priest was ready on the spot, a deacon was ready in England, and the first of the Wantage Sisters to be assigned for work abroad were preparing for the voyage to India. The widespread distress and famine gave an opening for the spread of the Gospel, through the number of starving children whose bodies and souls alike were ready to be cared for and fed. And so, "by the good hand of our God upon us," the opening was as complete as it could be, and the means, material and personal, were furnished exactly as they were needed. As yet the "Cowley Fathers" had nothing to do with the Mission: their first connection with it was the outcome of a later "Providence," by which the nascent Mission was saved from the perils which beset it when means were failing its promoters after two or three years of work.

The Mission was actually started towards the end of 1877, and Mr. Dulley and Mr. Rivington, the priest and the deacon just mentioned, took up their abode at Panch Howds; while the Sisters, fresh from England, were established in the neighbouring cantonment. The famine boys were installed at Panch Howds, and the girls were made over to the Sisters. The forlorn little S.P.G. Mission, located in the bazaars of the cantonment, was incorporated with the new one for the time being; and, at intervals, for several years, young missionaries of S.P.G. were received by Mr. Rivington and Mr. Dulley, while they worked for their vernacular examinations, and acquired some knowledge of the country. Thus a nucleus of Christianity was established on the outskirts of the heathen city; the children, as instructed and baptized, forming a centre for future development. A room in the Mission-house formed the chapel, and the Sisters, whose house was at a distance, had their services in a chapel of their own, or attended the neighbouring church. Within a few months of the first start, industrial work had been established, and the boys who were old enough to learn were being trained to support themselves as carpenters.

The character impressed upon the Mission in these its earliest days has been retained, and still forms its leading feature after thirty years of hard work.

A mere list of the works which it carries on may perhaps give a certain idea of the way in which the Mission has been blessed.

Putting aside two works outside, which happily are self-supporting—the nursing of the General Hospital and the care of St. Mary's Girls' School for English and Eurasian pupils—the institutions of the Mission proper comprise the following schools: The High School of St. John for boys, and that of the Epiphany for girls, both teaching up to the University Matriculation; St. Joseph's Workshop for carpenter boys, and St. Michael's Industrial School for girls; St. Pancras' School, the feeder of St. Joseph's Workshop; St.

Gabriel's School for girls, intermediate between the Epiphany High School and St. Michael's Industrial School; St. Elizabeth's Crêche for orphan and destitute babies, which feeds both St. Pancras' and St. Michael's, so far as the poor little starvelings can be rescued from early death. Besides these, there are a Cottage Hospital and a Dispensary, which are doing most useful work.

As far as the work of the Mission has been blessed and acknowledged by God, its fruits are attributed by the workers to the fact that their care and attention have been given, before all things else, to developing their central work; allowing the spread of the Gospel to follow under God's good Providence, as the, so to speak, natural sequence of the labour thus expended. The children brought in by the famine in 1876–7 formed the nucleus of the original Mission; their children are its mainstay to-day; their grandchildren — so rapidly, in India, does generation succeed generation — are growing up to swell its ranks. This must not be taken to mean that expansion and evangelisation have been things unknown in Poona under the care of the Panch Howds Mission. It has its roll of converts — a few from the ranks of the Brahmins, who count for so much in Poona. But the converts have been, for the most part, attracted by the inevitable influence which spreads as an aroma around a centre of Christian life. Among the conversions due, under God, in part at least, to this influence was that of the Pandita Ramabai.

The material extension of the Mission has been not its least striking feature. On a portion of the original compound stands the stately Church of the Holy Name—a Dedication which seemed to be called for because the quarter of the city which includes the Mission is dedicated, by name, to the Evil One—*Vetal Peyt*, or the devil's quarter—and the Holy Name of Jesus is to be read on the perforated vane which surmounts the bell-cote of the building. A grand campanile has been added, in which, for the first time in India, a peal of church bells is hung. The Sisters have buildings of their own within a stone's-throw of the original Mission-house. Another adjacent property has been bought as an addition to the boys' school, and three grades of schools for girls are housed in the Sisters' compound. There has hardly been a year of late which has not witnessed some development of the work, with a corresponding growth of *matériel*.

And in the spiritual development of the Mission there has been abundant cause for thanksgiving. Difficulties, of course, there have been, even scandals and heart-breaks sometimes—what work has ever been without them, however blessed by God? But growth, expansion, encouragement have been ever the order of things; till now the difficulty is to keep pace with the needs of the Mission as regards the supply of workers and the means by which they are to live.

Such are the practical developments of this concentrated Mission at Poona. They have resulted in establishing a community which, no doubt, is as far from being perfect as most communities are in this field of wheat and tares. But it is a blessed fact that, after thirty years of hard work, one can see in the Church of the Holy Name congregations as devout and attentive, and with as adequate a conception of worship, as can be found in any church where simple people worship in any town in England. The communicants number about two hundred. And if the standard of outward reverence be any indication at all of what lies beneath the surface, the reality of the Gift and of the blessing is keenly appreciated among them.

Nor does the concentration of the Mission mean the creation of dependent Christians, who look to their teachers for support. Industry and pecuniary self-reliance have been keynotes of the work from the first.

A word may be added, in conclusion, on the spiritual ideals of Panch Howds. The *personnel* of the clerical staff has changed more than once or twice since the Mission was first established. The first great development of work took place under the headship of Mr. Rivington, still a priest in the Bombay Diocese. To him succeeded Mr. Nanson, afterwards Principal of Bishop's College, Calcutta. Both these were associates of Cowley, though not belonging to the Order. Since Mr. Nanson left, the actual head of the Mission has always been a Father of St. John's—first, the saintly Father Relton, called home after an accident which befell him in the building of the campanile, and buried in the little cemetery where our native Christians lie. But whoever has been at the head, the ideals have never varied. The only conception of work which has ever prevailed in the Mission, among clergy and Sisters alike, has been that work for God must be, in the strictest sense, the outcome of personal devotion, the necessary, inevitable expression of a life wholly dedicated to the Saviour, and lived in the power of the Spirit. The original chapel in the Mission-house, with its humble, homely fittings, the splendid Church of the Holy Name, with its altar gorgeous with marbles, the chapels of the Sisters' houses—three of them altogether, two in the European cantonment, and one at Panch Howds itself—it is from the fervent devotions of these that everything practical has issued. Make yourself the shrine of the Spirit, and the Spirit will make of you a power in the hearts of others—this has been the guiding principle which has regulated the whole of the work from its first inception till now. No lower aim has been thought possible than to be the sheer instrument of God. No means have been regarded as admissible for carrying out that aim, but the power which comes of prayer, and of union with the Saviour in His Sacraments. When aught has been effected for God, it has been sought to offer it to Him with the humblest acknowledgments of unworthiness, and with an absolute reliance on His grace.

CHAPTER III

THE COMPARATIVE VALUE OF THESE TWO TYPES OF MISSION UNDER THE ACTUAL CONDITIONS OF INDIA

IT will be perfectly plain from the above that the experience of the present writer has made this his primary conviction on the subject of the two types of Mission—that the Diffused evangelistic efforts, which constitute the primary aim of the conventional type of Mission, depend for safety and soundness on the exact proportion and degree to which the aims of the Concentrated Mission are applied to supplement and to stiffen them.

But on this the question must arise, whether it were not the sounder procedure to follow the original order, as I have shown that it is found in the Acts. Can it often be the preferable order to form a large, scattered flock by diffusive and aggressive endeavour, and then to watch for the point where all one's methods must be altered, and a new first aim taken up; with all the innumerable risks of missing the golden moment, and complicating one's future work? Were it not wiser to begin at the centre, instead of rushing at once to the circumference; to devote one's earliest efforts, not to gathering in, far and wide, as many as will listen to the Gospel, but to forming a nucleus of Christianity? —a Christianity not widely evangelistic in its immediate, primary aims, but developed, deepened, intensified by continual effort and prayer; whose effects upon the heathen around might be, as at the birth of the Church, the spontaneous, inevitable outcome of the work of the Spirit within.

This method has its difficulties and its dangers; as what, indeed, has not in a world where the heavenly treasure is contained in earthen vessels? There is the danger of converting the Mission into a hotbed of well-meaning unreality, or a training-ground for conscious hypocrisy. This result is certain to follow unless a spirit of manly common sense pervade the whole work as an atmosphere; unless sentiment be absolutely banished; unless those at the head of the Mission are continually bearing it in mind that things which come naturally to themselves could only be rank affectation on the part of those whom they are training. For spontaneity and reality and simplicity are infinitely precious in themselves; while standards of external observance are then, and then only, to be valued when, unforced, unconscious, unalloyed, they form but an outward expression for grace worked into the character.

For an instance of the inevitable dangers which beset the Concentrated Mission, we have only to recur to the Acts. The case of Ananias and Sapphira will be found very greatly to the point. A standard was allowed to grow up—was made almost a matter of course—which our Lord during His earthly Ministry had treated as entirely exceptional. We can infer from the First Epistle to the Corinthians[1] how some were found very early who would exalt one counsel of perfection, the celibate life for God, into a binding rule for all Christians. Another, the parting with all, and the distributing of one's goods to the poor, seems to have grown so practically universal among the earliest converts to the Church that it elicited an attempt at its adoption from this unhappy pair, who had not the strength to live it out. It may be that, with conscious hypocrisy, they desired to get credit, from the first, for a degree of evangelical fervour which they knew that they did not possess. Or perhaps when they sold their possessions, they had formed a resolution about them which they had not the strength to fulfil. In any case the moral of the story is that a standard too high to be universal was allowed to be commonly adopted, and that two of the weaker sort fell victims to the spiritual pressure exerted by its general prevalence. They attempted to carry it out, or at least to get credit for doing so. They were led to lose their souls by the tendency which must always be present when even an attempt

[1] I Cor. VII. I indicates that St. Paul had been asked whether Christians might lawfully be married.

is being made to treat extraordinary devotion as the natural standard for Christians.

It may, then, be laid down very certainly that every Concentrated Mission, in India or anywhere else, will have to watch with unceasing vigilance against a danger inherent in its methods, one which claimed its earliest victims from among the first followers of Christ. Yet it would not be any more rational to condemn the system as a whole, on the ground of this danger besetting it, than to abolish a regular ministry because there was a traitor Apostle —who, alas! has had imitators enough.

Whatever be its dangers and drawbacks, the system of Concentrated Missions seems to have an especial suitability to the circumstances and idiosyncrasies of Hindus. For characters enfeebled by Caste, and debauched by Pantheistic idolatry, it surely must be the case that a long and careful training is needed as a precedent condition for developing Christian independence.

The one grand object, of course, which every evangelist must pursue, is the development of an indigenous Church which shall work upon lines of its own, taking nothing from European Christianity but the Bible, the Creeds, the Sacraments, and the historic Orders of the Ministry. The goal may lie centuries in front of us. At present it is not in sight, even dimly descried on the horizon. The single question for us is, How can we reach it most certainly? Not, How can we accelerate the running? —which indeed were the most fatal of mistakes— but, What are the steps in the present which will make for its ultimate attainment?

If God raise up native evangelists, all on fire with the kind of enthusiasm which has resulted again and again in marvellous revivals of Hinduism, then the future will lie in their hands. But it were not too much to affirm that the one grand anxiety of the present is to be found in the too patent fact that the Gospel, thus far, is an exotic; that it has shown little sign as yet of becoming so thoroughly assimilated by the best of our Indian converts as to prove a power in their hands for the Christianisation of the country. On the contrary, the almost universal tendency is for the bulk of the native converts to remain inactive, unprogressive, content to be Christians themselves without a thought of spreading the Faith. And, worse still, for the best of their number, who are fit for Holy Orders, and for work under foreign supervision, to fail of becoming independent, to show no sign, or hardly any, of developing leadership among their brethren.

It may sound, then, almost paradoxical to maintain that the Concentrated Mission, the devotion of the energies of missionaries to developing and building up their flocks, is the method adapted most perfectly to the conditions of Indian Christianity as found in the present day. Ought we not, it might possibly be asked, to devote ourselves to developing among them that spirit of aggressive endeavour in which they are so totally lacking?

I reply, without the smallest hesitation, that this most desirable consummation will be best and soonest reached by the endeavour to train up a few to be Christians in a deeper reality. It is, after all, on the average Christian that there depends, more than anything else, the prospect of a few being found who shall stand clean away from the rest, who shall grow into something quite different, into apostles to the mass of their countrymen. Get an adequate standard on the whole, and there will always be a few to rise above it. Let the general average be low, and, again, the better average just above it will prove correspondingly disappointing. And therefore our policy for the present is to work up the general level; being always carefully on the watch to see who come to the front, and can be raised to something higher themselves, to become, again, in the next generation, a starting-point for a higher mediocrity, out of which shall grow higher exceptions.

In the meantime Christian communities, living ordered lives of faith, bringing forth the fruits of that faith in a social and personal life contrasting with the heathen around, form the best and most persuasive of arguments for recommending the Gospel to their neighbours.

Bishop Johnson, late of Calcutta, whose twenty years as Metropolitan, in an age of railway travelling, have given him an experience of missions unique in the history of India, has repeatedly expressed his opinion that a mission must pass twenty years under the guidance of some one leader before it will develop its capacities as they might be and ought to be developed.

CHAPTER IV

HISTORICAL ILLUSTRATIONS OF THE WORKING OF THESE TWO TYPES OF MISSION IN INDIA —XAVIER, SCHWARTZ, AND CAREY

THE early history of Indian Missions forms, alas! one long object-lesson on the futility of diffused evangelisation, not stiffened by concentrated work.

It would not, I believe, be untrue to say that, since the days of St. Paul, no grander or more fascinating personality has been brought to bear upon the heathen than that of St. Francis Xavier. His shrine is visited to-day, after the lapse of three centuries and a half, not only by Roman Catholic Christians—a Viceroy of India among their number—but by Christians of other denominations; nay, by Hindus, Mahommedans, and Parsis: so widely diffused throughout India is the fame of his sanctified character. Out of a total of some eleven years devoted to missionary work, he spent about five in India, and those broken up still smaller by voyages to the farthest East. Yet he effected a great work, and that not only in converting lapsed Europeans: the number of his native converts must be reckoned by the hundred thousand. Still, his methods are the crucial example of total failure of concentration, of belief in quantity, not quality, of counting the numbers baptized, not of seeking to build up his neophytes in the faith and practice of the Gospel. He ranged over provinces and kingdoms, preaching with a fervour and a winningness unsurpassed, one might say unrivalled; sweeping converts by the thousand into his net. We have it on his own authority that once, in the kingdom of Travancore, he baptized ten thousand in a month; that he used to preach till his speech broke down, and baptize till his hands refused their office. The force of his magnetic personality served to scatter an invading host when his Christians were attacked by Mahommedans. The magic of his apostolic personality broke through all barriers of language, all strangeness of foreign thought; so that opponents gave way before him, and bystanders were converted by his arguments, when they were totally incapable of comprehending them.

Yet what is the result to-day? That the conversion of the country to Christianity is no nearer than it was when he left it, for anything that his followers have done; that they form but a Christian caste, unprogressive, incapable of evangelising, observing distinctions of caste within the body of the Christian Church; holding their own with a pathetic faithfulness among people of other creeds, but woefully low in their practice, and scandalously superstitious in their conceptions; afraid of the Hindu gods; and all but idolaters themselves in their veneration of the saints and their images.

A priest of the Anglican Church was accosted one day in Bombay by an English Roman Catholic gentleman:—"Can you direct me to the Jesuit church, Sir?" —The Jesuit obedience, be it observed, is totally distinct from the Goanese in Roman Catholic India to-day. Having got the direction which he wanted, he added, to explain his request:—"I went to service last Sunday in there"—pointing to the Goanese church —"and I can never go there again: it was sheer idolatry, Sir."

I was once told by a friend in Bombay that an idol had been set up in his compound by one of his Hindu servants, and that he meant to have it taken away. "Shall you send —— to remove it, then?" naming a Goanese Christian servant. "Send him!" replied the owner of the compound. "Why, no Goanese dare touch it. I shall send a Mussulman to remove it."

Now many of the vices of method which paralysed Xavier's work for being either progressive or aggressive were inherent, no doubt, in his creed. He had a faith in the virtue of baptism, simply, *ex opere operato*, which led him to administer that sacrament as I have heard of its being administered by a Jesuit priest of to-day. This priest had been visiting a

Hindu in a hospital, and had made some preliminary attempts to put Christianity before him. The man died suddenly one night, and a missionary of the S.P.G., on visiting a Christian in the ward, was told to his great astonishment that the Jesuit had baptized the Hindu after he had passed into total unconsciousness. He asked him how he could do it on evidence quite insufficient to show that the man had desired it. "How could I tell," said the Jesuit, "that he had not the rudiments of faith and repentance?" If not to be positively known to be *without* the needful qualifications is taken by a Jesuit of to-day as constituting readiness for baptism, it is not difficult, perhaps, to divine why Xavier's Mission has yielded no better results.

But, indeed, we have his own authority for saying what his methods were. He started at a terrible disadvantage; for thousands of pearl fishers, who were heathens, had been baptized for political reasons; without any knowledge on their part except that submission to the rite—to which they attached no meaning—would secure them protection from Portugal in their quarrels with their Mussulman neighbours. As far as they were concerned right methods were almost precluded. For Xavier had to do what he could to bring the leading truths of Christianity within the reach of these poor creatures, baptized before his arrival. But even when working for himself, unhampered by previous sacrilege, he would preach to crowds of heathens; attract them by his personal magnetism till they were ready for anything he might propose; teach them the Commandments, the Creed, and some other verbal devotions, chiefly to the Mother of our Lord. And then, when they knew these by heart, he would admit them to the Church by baptism, and leave them to the care of others, who had none of his own unique force; then go off to repeat the same process in another, and yet many other places.

One would have thought that the most fervid enthusiast, with the profoundest faith in the sacraments, would have made some allowance at least for the circumstances of the country in which he was; that he would have asked whether the character of the people, their surroundings, their training, their beliefs were such as to justify the assumption that such preparation was sufficient.[1] But as far as his history shows, Xavier never was troubled with such a thought.

[1] Father Coleridge's *Life of Xavier* belongs to the type of hagiography thus described by Father Tyrrel, in his book *The Faith of the Millions*:—

"The old time-honoured saint's life, with its emphasis on the miraculous and startling features of the portrait, its suppression of what was natural, ordinary, and therefore presumably uninteresting, and consequently its abandonment of all attempt to weave the human and divine into one truthful and harmonious whole, showing the gradual evolution of the perfect from the imperfect, to many minds makes no appeal whatever."

Sir James Stephen's portrait of the great Jesuit missionary, in his

I shall have to draw out, further on, what it was that may have weighed with him, as it has done, in a lesser degree, with many a missionary since, to make him hold that methods like these were formed on apostolic example. Suffice it to have indicated now how woefully, in the case of the Goanese, experience has proved to the Church that the inference could not be justified. Even methods so unsatisfactory as those of the Society of Jesus have had very different results in other countries than India, where to the vices inherent in their system they have not added another by leaving the new-made converts to develop their Christian life with inadequate subsequent assistance; where they have not spread their missions over a range which was absolutely prohibitive to the deepening and confirming of faith.

The next grand, fervid personality which emerges in the Indian field is that of the Lutheran, Schwartz, who worked over much the same ground. The Danish-Indian Missions, to the undying credit of Denmark, had been established and genuinely worked for nearly fifty years before Schwartz went

Essays in Ecclesiastical Biography, is conceived and executed in his most brilliant manner, and leaves on the mind a clear-cut impression which makes his sketch more telling than many a lengthy biography. With the Jesuit and the system which he represents the brilliant writer has, of course, little sympathy. Of the elemental greatness of the character, and the depth of the fervid devotion brought to bear, for God, on man's welfare, his appreciation is generous and thoroughgoing.

to the country in 1750. To that one Power in Europe had it appeared, since Xavier's days, that mercantile relations with India, still more that territorial occupation, carried with them this duty to the natives.

The early Danish missionaries had done some solid work. Schwartz found a Lutheran community, the number of whose Indian converts had amounted to some eight thousand; with a Tamil translation of the Bible, and with all the ordinary appliances which necessarily grow up round a mission. There had been no grand, commanding character among the earlier Danish missionaries, to be compared with Schwartz himself, but there had been men of sufficient power, and of sufficient personal devotion, to have laid a deep foundation.

If only their greater successor had confined himself to building on that, content to leave wider extensions to follow in later years, the ultimate results of his work might have answered to the grandeur of his character. But not even powers and goodness like those which he brought to his work could secure for it depth or permanence under the methods which he actually followed. He extended the range of his work from some way north of Madras to Tinnevelly in the farthest south, and even to parts of Ceylon—with the result that after his death his missions collapsed altogether.

He died in 1798, leaving large congregations of Christians scattered everywhere throughout this vast region. And when, in 1825, the remains of some of his work were taken over by the S.P.G., they found whole villages and congregations from which the knowledge of the Gospel had almost entirely disappeared. The people still called themselves Christians. But of what being Christians meant they had lost the rudimentary idea. Here and there a few of the older would gather for prayer and reading, but there were places where Christianity was extinct. Xavier's Goanese converts at least left Christian descendants, imperfect as is their Christianity. Even this were too much to affirm of many of Schwartz's people.

Yet his work, as he did it himself, and as others did it in his lifetime, was far from being superficial. It is plain that he was scrupulously particular in demanding of all his converts real evidence of faith and repentance before he admitted them to baptism. He tells us of instances of devotion, of exemplary life and piety, which can leave no doubt upon the mind that he really had brought people to Christ, and that in very large numbers.

The personal character of the man was enough to account for his successes. Commanding in the force of his will, he was as simple and humble as a child. A celibate on true Gospel principles, "for the sake of the Kingdom of Heaven," he had a nature tenderly sympathetic, which entered with touching affection into the family lives of his friends. A missionary to the exclusion of all else, he displayed such forcefulness and such tact in his dealings with English rulers and with native chiefs alike, that he was employed—could not help being employed—in the most delicate political negotiations; "The Christian," as they fondly called him, being the only European in the country who was absolutely trusted by the natives. During a fierce triangular warfare between the English Government at Madras, the Hindu Rajah of Tanjore, and the fierce Mahommedan Nawab who was in power at Seringapatam, he was allowed by all alike to have access to their capitals and their forts. He was allowed to preach the Gospel on the ramparts of Seringapatam, when engaged on a political embassy; and that, when it was known to the Mussulman that the English, who had sent him on the embassy, were playing false behind the back of their ambassador! When the misrule of the chief of Tanjore led his subjects to desert him by thousands, and take refuge in another State, he sent Schwartz to win them back. They returned at the instance of "The Christian." And, again, when Tanjore was to be invested, and no one would victual the fort, because no one could hope that he would be paid, "The Christian" was sent by the Chief to negotiate with the recalcitrant merchants, with the result that provisions came in to the satisfaction of contractors and of Chief. When the end of his life arrived, the Chief, not a

Christian himself, wept over him as more than a father.[1]

The subsequent collapse of his work can only be attributed, then, to some radical fault in his methods.

Undoubtedly, both the Jesuit and the Lutheran must have thought that in all that they did they were following the model of St. Paul. The Apostle, they would certainly have said, ranged over vast tracts in two continents, founding Churches wherever he went. He did not stop, they might have argued, to ask whether his children in Christ would be able to maintain themselves in the faith when his personal presence was withdrawn: he trusted to the grace which they had received; he left them to work out their salvation by the help of the Spirit of God; revisiting them occasionally, as he could, and communicating with them by letter. Why should not his successors do the like?

A generalisation such as this from the methods of the first great evangelist has undoubtedly much to be said for it on broad and general grounds. But

[1] Dean Pearson's *Life of Schwartz* is a rather ponderous specimen of the conventional evangelical biography. It chronicles the life of the great Lutheran with a hearty appreciation of its piety. It brings out the power of the man by a record of what he effected, which is patient, faithful, and unexaggerated. But the touch is heavy and the style uninteresting. One gets no vivid portrait of the man, and criticism is not attempted. No defects in the handling of the subject could render the character of Schwartz aught else but lovable and interesting, but 'tis pity that he had not a biographer who could handle the chronicle of facts in a manner more inspiring and inspired.

there was one disastrous exception to be remembered in dealing with India. There is one Epistle of St. Paul which does not begin with thanksgiving. About the state of the Galatian Church he could not rejoice before God. A different Gospel—a no-Gospel—had crept in to seduce them from Christ. The method which had prospered elsewhere had disastrously failed among them. The withdrawal of his personal presence from converts of a barbarous race with a poor reputation for stability, far removed from civilising influences, had proved to be a shock to their faith against which they could not stand. They fell victims to the first false teachers who offered them a plausible Judaism in place of the Gospel of Christ.

Nor is it only from one of his Epistles that we find how the method of St. Paul, as applied in the case of the Galatians, proved unsuitable for barbarous people. Ever after the Divine interposition on which I have commented so fully in the chapter on Method as such, he confined the whole of his work to people whose circumstances and whose training made them fit to be evangelised and left. The Hellenised, educated communities on either side of the Ægean; with Roman law in full force; with the culture, intellectual and moral, which Greek civilisation afforded; to whom, again, in time of need, a Timothy could be sent with a letter, a Titus with personal explanations—these, and not uncivilised

Celts, not Bithynians far from the centre, form the subject of his subsequent labours. The disastrous mistake of Galatia had been summarily "hindered" from repetition: the lesson had been learnt once for all.

It is not surprising, perhaps, that a Xavier or a Schwartz never learnt it. The first had but five years of India. The second, through his well-nigh half-century, was continually revisiting his converts, and sustaining them in what he had taught them. Yet both were pioneers in the country; so that they never acquired the *data* for learning their lesson in full. We ourselves, after three centuries and a half, are but learning for ourselves and our successors, how Caste, that deadliest enemy with which the Gospel must grapple in India, has riveted on the necks of the people the yoke of Pantheistic idolatry; how morals are debauched by idolatry, and minds are enfeebled by Pantheism; how character, as found in the individual, is stunted, distorted, enfeebled, by the positiveness of a mere group-morality. Small wonder that neither Xavier nor Schwartz could realise how character, morals, religion, thought must be patiently trained and formed, under age-long teaching of the Gospel, before the Christianity of India could become a spontaneous growth; before it could cease to be exotic; before the necessity could end for its being cultivated, tended, nursed by Europeans constantly on the spot. In a word, it took a

Xavier and a Schwartz to spend and to be spent over mistakes, to give their lives to splendid failure, before the right methods for India could begin to be generalised or realised.

The lives, then, of these great pioneers, the Jesuit and the Lutheran alike, have one grand lesson to teach us—how not even the noblest of personalities unsupported by adequate method can contend, with ultimate success, against the essential difficulties which Hinduism presents to the evangelist.

What is meant by an adequate method may be briefly presented as follows. In dealing with consciences and characters which are moulded directly by Caste, and which express in their every development the religious and philosophical systems of which Caste is the social outcome, the one grand essential is this—a mean must be accurately struck between the slavish obedience to a system, which Caste has but rendered too easy, and that premature grant of full liberty, which must lead to inevitable licence in lives unprepared for its exercise.

And such a system, again, can never be adequately implanted if the topographical area of a mission be extended too widely for prudence. Of this last so necessary precaution neither Xavier nor Schwartz had a thought. It may have been humility, perhaps, which kept each from realising for a moment how his own enthusiastic work, with its enormous geographical range, must fall into weaker hands when its Founder should pass to his rest. Looking back to the history which they made, we can see how the inevitable break—between genius and ordinary ability—was bound to prove speedily fatal.

In this particular respect, then, in the over-extension of their work, they each made the same mistake. Their failures to attain the due mean between passive obedience and liberty were exactly the opposite to one another. With the Jesuit, it was Method run mad, the substitution of mechanical formulæ for adequate conceptions of Christianity, with its personal development of the spirit. With the Lutheran, it was absence of Method; it was reliance on the power of the Gospel to develop spiritual independence in characters quite unprepared for it.

Who, then, first gathered the fruits of these centuries of noble mistakes?

If the honour of being the earliest pioneer belongs to a Spaniard and a Jesuit, and if the next commanding personality is that of a German Lutheran, sent out under the auspices of Denmark, the credit of the first great advance towards solving the problem of Method can be claimed for a countryman of our own. Not, alas! for our National Church; for Carey, the father, as he is called, of modern missions in India, belonged to the Baptist persuasion.

If ever a Heaven-sent genius wrought a conquest over obstacles and disabilities, it was here, in this humbly-born Englishman. Not only was he born in low station—his father was a parish clerk—but he received hardly any education. When he came upon a Greek quotation in a book which he was struggling to master, he had to carry the unknown characters to be deciphered by a broken-down scholar who lived some miles from his home. And this man, before he died, took part in translating the Bible into some forty languages or dialects, Chinese among the number! He started in life as a cobbler—would never let any one claim for him the more dignified title of shoemaker—he died a professor of Sanskrit, the honoured friend and adviser of the Government whose earliest greeting, when he landed on the shores of the country, had been to prohibit him from preaching. He founded a notable college for the training of native missionaries. And he added to his other accomplishments an extraordinary practical knowledge of horticulture and arboriculture.—"When I am gone," he said sadly on his death-bed, "Brother Marshman will let in the cows to trample down my garden." And he was a naturalist in other departments. Besides his attainments as a student, the man was so eminently practical that when forbidden to live as a missionary within British territories in India, he settled to the charge of a plantation, and made use of his leisure time in acquiring a knowledge of the people, and fitting himself for future opportunities. Such a nature's gentleman was he that he married as his second wife a Danish lady of title, and attached her fervently and for life to her peasant-bred English husband. And even more striking than this, he combined all the missionaries who worked with him, with all their wives and families, into a large domestic community, who had but one household in common. Most, or all of them, were of the artisan class. They were living in the climate of Bengal, where, as many an Englishman knows, every petty occasion of dissension will magnify itself to the point of exasperation. They had the usual children and servants to complicate their domestic relations. And they lived in peace and affection as one great Christian family. In what words shall we celebrate the tact which held them all together? And he possessed such power of concentration that when his poor first English wife, who never was fitted for India, went into a violent mania, he could care for her with a husband's devotion, and yet carry on his own studies in a room where her ravings could be heard.

But the one grand merit of Carey, without which his marvellous qualities had been lost like those of his predecessors, was that he, with the intuition of genius, set to work instinctively, from the first, on the lines of the Concentrated Mission. There was no diffusion of his energies over impossible tracts of country and impracticable numbers of converts. A few really Christianised people, with the means of future extension—this he seems to have set before him as his object. He left no great body of converts, but he laid a solid foundation, to be built on by those who should succeed him. His college—at Danish Serampore, his refuge, when his countrymen expelled him—is at work to-day, training missionaries. And the Baptist persuasion as a whole retains the missionary spirit which he was used to implant among its members. Above all, his translations of the Scriptures formed a basis for the many versions which followed in progressive improvement. To appreciate this service in its fulness, one must know the toil which it entails to secure a first version at all, and the efforts, year after year, which successive generations have to make, before the genius of a language is finally caught and expressed; to say nothing of the snares and the pitfalls which betray the first translators—the hideous allusive vocabulary which permeates a heathen tongue, and may besmirch some God-given text with foul associations of lubricity, to be discovered by horror-stricken revisers after years of unsuspecting use.

I should hardly be saying too much, did I lay down that subsequent Missions have proved to be successful, or the opposite, in a proportion fairly exact to their adoption of Carey's methods. More than one great missionary genius was directly indebted to him, and to the Baptist Community at Serampur. Our own grand Henry Martyn betook himself thither for inspiration. And one of the most touching scenes in the missionary history of India is that in which the fiery Duff, the founder of Educational Missions, strode up from the landing-place at Serampur to the room where the aged Carey was waiting to welcome and bless him. We read of the little, sallow old man who tottered with faltering steps to salute his ruddy young visitor, and of how, after a long conversation, he dismissed him with the parting hope, that while much had been said of Dr. Carey, the one and only Name which he would put before the youth of Calcutta might be that of Dr. Carey's Saviour.

What heart of a true English Churchman will refuse to be thrilled with sympathy over the meeting of the Baptist with the Presbyterian? Nay, what cheek will not blush with shame? The chief contribution of our Church to the Mission which Carey started had been the sneer of Sydney Smith about the band of "converted cobblers" who had gone to evangelise India. At least let us recall with thankfulness that the help of our oldest Society, that for the Promotion of Christian Knowledge, had been freely extended to Schwartz, when the Church as a whole was doing nothing.

CHAPTER V

ON ONE SPECIAL DEVELOPMENT OF THE CONCENTRATED FORM OF MISSION—THE EDUCATIONAL MISSION

THE concentrated form of mission, about which I have written at length, has known several forms of development. One of these, the Educational Mission, as originated by Duff in Calcutta, and reproduced in other places by other and lesser men, calls for special and detailed treatment.

When Duff arrived in Calcutta, in 1830, education, in any real sense, was not to be found in India. Of the total population of Bengal, the most civilised province in the country, 92½ per cent are believed to have been absolutely illiterate. The possibility of a woman being educated had never so much as been thought of; but even of the more favoured sex, only about 16 per cent were able to read and write. And such education as there was among either Mahommedans or Hindus had been confined to Oriental languages and to the literary and theological classics recognised by their systems respectively. How far even educated people had been touched by European ideas may be estimated from a single fact—that the first scientific conception which Duff had to communicate to his pupils, who belonged to the most intelligent classes, was that rain was not to be accounted for by the spouting of a celestial elephant discharging the water from his trunk!

And even the efforts of Government to impart education to the people on the lines of their own religions had been total failures in practice. Great editions of Indian classics, produced at the public cost, had been left on the warehouse shelves because no one would take them at a gift. Not only the professors in the colleges were paid for lecturing upon them : the students were paid for listening, and were hardly procurable at that. The Hindus had started a college for teaching their own young men, and the favourite subjects for learning were the principles of Tom-Paine atheism, carried out to the moral results which Europe associates with them.

But if there was no education in the actual India of the day, things were ripe for its introduction ; the very atmosphere was vibrating with the thought of it.

Trevelyan, in his Commissionership at Delhi, was brooding over plans for introducing it : his future brother-in-law, Macaulay, was Secretary to the Board of Control, and was soon to proceed to India as a member of the Viceroy's Council. The Governor-General of the day was no other than Lord William Bentinck, a man of the most enlightened views, ever ready for any scheme which would work for the welfare of the people. And, perhaps more important than all, the great theistic reformer, Rajah Rammohun Roy, was at work among the Brahmins of Calcutta, urging them to educate their sons, and himself initiating the work; exposing the absurdities of Hinduism, and preaching an eclectic religion; stopping, alas! far short of Christianity, but forming a *præparatio evangelica* invaluable as a stepping-stone for Duff.

Into the train thus sensitively laid the glorious personality of the missionary fell suddenly like a spark from Heaven. If ever an opportunity and a man were divinely brought together, it was when Duff set foot in Calcutta. He had been shipwrecked twice on the way; once off the Cape of Good Hope, and again in the treacherous Hooghly, with its shoals and its tremendous tideway. And something of the awful regard which St. Paul excited at Malta, when he shook off the snake into the fire, became associated in the native mind with this man, twice saved from the waters.

But the character of the fiery Highlander needed no supernatural halo to make it stand out before all men. Its greatness was patent at a glance. It was my privilege, as a child of seven, to be frequently petted at his knees, and I heard his farewell sermon, in the little Free Kirk of Moulin, before his last start for Calcutta. At this day, after more than half a century, there stands out clear before my mind the recollection of the spiritual intensity, the profound absorption in work, the magnetic power over hearts, the large-hearted genial buoyancy, which appealed to even a child with the sense that our venerable friend was a very king among men.

Like all transcendent characters, he was partly the product of his age, partly the power which transformed it. The spirit of Missions was abroad in the Established Church of Scotland. The opposition with which it was met had been not only stolid, but presumptuous—had actually ventured to voice itself, at an official meeting of a Presbytery, with the assertion that missions to the heathen were not, in that day at least, to be regarded as part of God's plan; that His Church was under no obligation to work for the conversion of the world; but that she was rather to acquiesce fatalistically in the present limitations of her borders. But Chalmers, with others like-minded, had triumphed over even such obstacles; and when Duff was ordained to the ministry the opportunity was waiting for the man. He landed from his marvellous voyaging not entirely, in intention at least, a free agent for the work entrusted to him, but with a spirit so autonomous and so determined that he brushed aside on the spot the only restriction laid upon him. He had been told to do much as he pleased, except that the city of Calcutta was not to be the sphere of his labours:

he plunged at once into work in that city—never worked, indeed, anywhere else! For a struggle with organised Brahminism such as he was prepared to undertake he felt that there could be but one field—the metropolis of the country which it terrorised. Its official head-quarters might be elsewhere; Calcutta was the centre of life, and therefore, in the long run, of religion.

He found an ally from the first in Rajah Rammohun Roy, who lent him a room for his school. And on that room, and on the school which he opened there, his work all turned as on its pivot.

His conception of it was marvellously noble. People's minds being ripe for education, he would take all the knowledge of Europe as a point of departure for the Gospel. The earliest inceptions of education should be made with Christ as their goal. All the literature, the philosophy, the science which Christian Europe had gained should be placed within reach of Hindus, and all should lead up to Christ, "in Whom are hid all the treasures of wisdom and knowledge." To be an enlightened man and to be a believing Christian should be, in the minds of his pupils, but one thing from two points of view. Development, moral and spiritual—the development of Christian character under the guidance of the Spirit of God—should be presented to India from the first as the end and the scope of education.

The idea was worthy of the man. And it seemed,

for a time at least, as though the practical results were to be worthy the idea and its originator.

The boys embarked on their schooling in a spirit of fervid enthusiasm, and many of the scruples of their parents were surmounted by Rammohun Roy. He himself, he used to tell them, had studied the sacred books of Mahommedanism and Buddhism and Christianity; while yet, in point of keeping caste, he had remained an orthodox Hindu. The missionary was too fervidly honest to make any concealment of his purpose. If he offered a European education, he offered it as a step towards the Gospel. But even so the craving for knowledge overcame all scruples for a time. The party of conservatism at any price was, of course, arrayed against him. He had the honour, unique in mission history, of being threatened by Hindu alarmists with the hoisting of a quarantine flag outside the door of his lecture-room, as a warning of the danger of frequenting it. Yet frequented it continued to be. And enlightenment, and presently conversions began to obtain among his scholars. The quality of the neophytes was undeniable. They turned out, in the ultimate result, the most uniformly satisfactory converts ever known in an Indian mission. In the early stages, indeed, the ungoverned enthusiasm of some of them—not, certainly, of the most satisfactory—produced very real embarrassments, upon which I need not dwell. But the Cross was borne by others with unflinching constancy and courage. There were terrible scenes of wailing outside the great Missionary's house, as boys who were preparing for baptism withstood the impassioned entreaties of fathers and mothers and caste-fellows. There were even awful cases of the relatives of inquirers or catechumens endeavouring to save their sons from abandoning Caste for Christianity by leading them into horrible vices, in the hope that indulgence in these would make them abhorrent to their teacher.

Had Duff been made of cast iron, or had he been superior to the weakness, so common in missionary enthusiasts, of forgetting that, after all, he had a body, and that his work must depend on his taking care of it, there is no saying where he need have stopped. As it was, he ran himself to a standstill, and was forced to withdraw from India; though the results of his self-sacrificing labours were permanent both in Scotland and in Calcutta. The enthusiasm and the permanent interest which he continued to create at home go on to the present day. And, amid all the sordid worldliness, the mere care for material advantage, which characterise educated youth in the India of the present day, there still survives in Calcutta some veritable passion for learning, some disinterested appreciation of culture, to be found in no other of its cities—all which have come down to the present by direct descent from Duff, and from his handful of early converts.

Such was the Educational Mission in its origin and

earliest inception. It has been worked by many men in many parts of India since Duff broke down in health, and was obliged to abandon it himself. There has been no other case in which its results have been the same. Much allowance, no doubt, must be made for the difference so often felt between the genius and enthusiasm of a founder and the ability and earnestness of successors.

But there are weaknesses inherent in the method, even in hands such as those of Duff. To begin with, its effect upon the students can never be all that he looked for, except in a minority of cases. To that fervid servant of God, to be a thoroughly cultivated man was inseparable from being a Christian. To him, intellectual culture was but part of a larger whole, the spiritual character of the man. To him, the end of education was "to present every man faultless before God." But with his students this could not be the case. A few of them were so permeated with his spirit that they were led to assimilate his ideals. But even to the average Christian to be intellectually cultured is one thing, and to serve God fervently is another. How soon, then, must heathens have learnt that they could assimilate what Duff had to teach of Western literature and science, and leave altogether aside their master's love for Christ.

And when such is the case with a student, what effect must be produced on his character by the mere intellectual assimilation of the deepest Christian truths?—for with nothing short of this did Duff imbue his pupils, at least on the intellectual side. He did not take as his model the addresses in the Acts of the Apostles, with all the reserve which obtained when the truth was being urged on non-Christians. Nothing less than the Epistles of St. Paul and the Gospel according to St. John would serve him for teaching Hindus. Had he confined himself in ordinary cases to enforcing the holiness of God and the need of a Saviour from sin; had he reserved all teaching more advanced for those who were spiritually awake to it, and could assimilate it to the saving of their souls, he had been truer to Apostolic methods, and had set a less dangerous precedent.

What he actually introduced into India was a system easy to copy in slavish adherence to detail, impossible for any but himself to follow with ultimate safety. It has resulted in colleges and schools being opened all over the country, where the bribe of a cheap education is offered to Hindu youth, to induce them to submit every day to instruction in the Christian faith—which they have not a thought of accepting. Converts have been made in them, no doubt. A Wilson in Bombay, a Millar in Madras, a Noble at Masulipatam, could not bring their powers to bear without conversions ensuing. But it is unquestionable that the results of their work have included the production, by the hundred, of men whose knowledge of Christianity has drawn them no nearer to Christ. Such are less, not more, prepared to approach Him as penitent sinners for having learnt the mysteries of the Gospel while unconscious of needing a Saviour.

Again, all these bad results have been aggravated to a terrible degree by the competition of the Government system. When Duff first started in Calcutta he was working without a rival. To-day there are Government Universities in all the Presidency cities, and in other centres as well; while over the whole of India there are colleges and schools innumerable, in which all Western culture is brought within reach of the people. Nor is this Western culture cast always, or even generally, in any Christian mould. The English professors may be Christians; they may be absolutely indifferent; they may teach dogmatic atheism. Christian teaching with proselytising intent our Government, it is true, could not give. If it did it would be false to its pledges, and would be in danger of raising a rebellion. But the result of this secular system is an utter uprooting and disturbing of the students' religious convictions, while nothing is substituted for them. It is the constant complaint of fathers that their sons lose all belief in the religious systems of their ancestors, and are offered no other to replace them.

In competing with colleges like these, the heads of the missionary colleges are compelled, in self-defence, to try to underbid them pecuniarily. What effect is likely to be produced if a boy is set in the morning to read the Epistles of St. Paul, because by consenting to do so he will get his degree somewhat cheaper; while his teacher dare ask no questions as to which of the gods of the heathen he may worship in the afternoon?

But besides this effect on the students, there is a heavy count against the system from the point of view of missionaries themselves, and of those who send them out. If a young man lands in the country all on fire with missionary earnestness, and finds from his first arrival that the best of his time every day is occupied in teaching for degrees; that the lesson in the Christian religion need hardly form more than an episode in a day of secular teaching; that he can occupy the whole of his time in hard and praiseworthy work which has nothing to do with the Gospel, how long will his early enthusiasm survive this absorption of his energies?

With a Valpy French it may be different. After several years of work as head of a school such as this, he could gravely tell a young colleague: "I can work sixteen hours a day, but for one newly landed in India, perhaps fourteen will suffice while this hot-weather vacation lasts." It is plain that secular teaching meant no interference, for him, with the spiritual side of his work. But neither the intellectual power nor the spiritual fervour of a French is to be found in the ordinary missionary.

It has often occurred to the writer as he passed some stately building, the home of a missionary college—How would those who raised it with their pence regard this goodly pile, did they realise the proportion of its time which is spent on evangelisation as compared with secular studies?

To the credit of the S.P.G., it has kept itself above the temptations to which other societies have succumbed, and has refused to spend its funds on schools for secular education. It has also made strict rules for separating Christians and heathens in the daily instructions of its agents. I cannot say quite as much in favour of the Sister Society. The Cambridge Mission at Delhi gives a large proportion of its energies to imparting a university education without, as far as I know, any loss of spiritual power or undue diversion of energy. But the Oxford Mission at Calcutta seems to me to have solved the problem more nearly than any other society. It has no college or school. It is not an educational mission. But its missionaries devote much time to the welfare of native students by helping them morally and spiritually, and even by assisting them in their studies. Under the Indian university system hundreds of Hindu youths, from every part of the country, are thrown into the bazaars unprotected, and are left to shift for themselves, as regards all care for their characters, till the *dis*repute of a neighbourhood is what renders it attractive as a lodging-place. To boys thus utterly uncared for the Mission opens its doors. It has established a hostel for them, where they may live the lives of Hindus, only having opportunities afforded them of forming acquaintance with the missionaries, and of learning from intimacy with them what the Christian religion means.

PART III

RESULTS AND PROSPECTS

CHAPTER I

RESULTS—PRELIMINARY CONSIDERATIONS

THE question might well be raised, how far either Results or Prospects come fairly within the scope of this book. Yet Methods and Principles alike have to be tested in the light of their Results. And Prospects are what we have in view when we lay down Methods of working.

Before dealing with results in the past, there are several preliminary considerations which it is necessary at any rate to touch upon.

First comes the gigantic influence of heredity and age-long tradition, which, vast as it must be in any country, holds a place in the Indian equation unsurpassed, it may be unequalled. I have tried in earlier chapters to show the tremendous leverage which Hinduism exerts on individuals by the homogeneity of its System, intellectual, religious, and social.

I would add one or two illustrations to bring out its power over the race.

Seven centuries before Christ came, the Brahminical System of India had produced, or reacted into, Buddhism, a system which has often been described as dominating one-third of the world. This estimate is exaggerated, no doubt; but the fact that it should ever have been made will indicate the greatness of the Daughter to whom the Hindu Mother gave birth.

Where is Buddhism in the India of to-day? It is simply an historical expression. It has no place in India proper, but only in the borderland of Thibet—and, of course, in the Province of Burma, which is not a portion of India except for political purposes.

In the census of the Bombay Presidency, in 1891, the Buddhist religion was represented by a single adherent, and he, no doubt, a stranger from Ceylon; for in the streets of the Presidency town there had been seen, about that time, the masculine comb and petticoat of a travelling Cingalese trader.

The first time I visited the Caves of Karli, a gigantic Buddhist cave-temple, older than the Christian era, there was seated within the cave, as the only worshipper visible, an ash-besmeared Hindu devotee, reciting after the fashion of his kind the names of the Hindu gods. The last time I visited the place, the steps of a Hindu temple, hard by the Buddhist cave, were being washed, and wiped with her hair by a female Hindu pilgrim, while the cave was deserted altogether—a striking acted parable of the fate of the Buddhist religion in the country which gave it birth. The problem is yet unsolved, how Brahminism secured its victory. Did it exterminate the adherents of Buddhism, or did it absorb them into itself? Whatever the answer may be, the fact remains indisputable that a religion born in India is the faith of the masses to-day in Thibet, in Burma, in Ceylon, and, partially, in China and Japan; while in India it is simply extinct, and its very disappearance has disappeared, so that none knows how it took place.

And the Creed thus aggressive for destruction can modify other religions, till it extinguishes their leading characteristics, and can adapt itself to the ways of other Creeds till it puts on the very details of their worship. It has modified Indian Mahommedanism: it has adopted the very *cultus* of Romanism. A missionary known to me once accosted a Mahommedan devotee who was worshipping at the shrine of a *Pir*—a local saint of his Creed—and inquired of him what he was doing. "This is our god," was the reply—from the mouth of a professor of Monotheism in one of its strictest forms. And there is a celebrated shrine of the Madonna at Bandora, near Bombay, where Hindu women make offerings, to propitiate the so-called goddess, and obtain from her the gift of fecundity. Her image is adorned with jewels presented by Hindu pilgrims. They worship at the shrine of Xavier, when his remains are periodically exposed. The Good Friday rites at Thanna, where life-sized images on cars are dragged about the streets, attract many Hindu worshippers, and have themselves an idolatrous character. It is in dealing with a system such as this, with its power of adaptability and of absorption, that missionary results must be obtained.

Another consideration to be reckoned with is the effect upon the Hindu mind of the presence of Christians in India. And here I would beg of my readers to dismiss once for all from their thoughts the impressions possibly received from exaggerated words on platforms, or unguarded expressions in pamphlets, as well as from the fascinating stories of Mrs. Steel and Mr. Kipling. It is certainly not the case that the tone of English Society is a demoralising scandal to Hindus. I repeatedly inquired of a well-known Governor of Bombay what he thought of the picture presented in Mr. Kipling's word-pictures of Indian life. He replied, "I can only tell you that in my own experience the moral tone of society is higher in Bombay than in London." No one, of course, would affirm that the surroundings of a military cantonment in any part of India will offer a favourable impression of the moral results of Christianity. Take thousands of lusty young men, crowd them together in barracks, and keep them in compulsory celibacy, and they will not be a living epistle to commend Christianity to the heathen. Again, English Society in India, it must be frankly admitted, is openly and confessedly secular in tone. How, indeed, could it possibly be otherwise? Aged people are absolutely unknown: every British resident in India looks to end his days in England. Young children there are, up to six: from six to sixteen there are none. Thus the two great steadying influences of care for the aged and for the young are withdrawn from the British resident. Add to this that he is "putting in his time" in a country where he never will settle, and in which even his temporary sojourn may be divided among many stations; that he is contending with the enervating influences of a climate both foreign and deadly; that political interests are unknown under the sway of a benevolent despotism; that intellectual and literary pursuits cannot flourish in the absence of libraries—and it will hardly be matter for wonder that the rage for constant amusement which pervades the England of to-day obtains in an exaggerated form among our countrymen in the Indian Empire.

And, again, when people leave their homes they become more entirely themselves, are far less dominated by convention than they are in their native country. It follows quite naturally from this that those who were occasional communicants when they lived in a parish in England are only occasional church-goers when they have spent a few years in India; while those who were occasional church-goers neglect Public Worship altogether. They may spend a great part of their time at a distance from all means of grace, and so learn to disregard them *in toto.* Or they may only be visited by a chaplain some three or four times a year, and may depend for all other opportunities on the reading of prayers now and then by a layman from among themselves.

In a directly religious form, then, the influence of Englishmen in India is not wholly favourable to Missions. Indirectly and on the moral side, it would be true to affirm just the opposite. The influence of the English *Raj* is all on the side of what is elevating.

Never, perhaps, in the history of the world has there existed so grand a bureaucracy as that which administers India—incorruptible, devoted to duty, maintaining before the eyes of the natives an official standard of conscientiousness, to praise which were almost an impertinence. And this, be it remembered, among a people whose notion of equity in a Judge is accepting bribes from both sides, to be returned in the case of the loser. So incomprehensible, indeed, to the average native mind, is our standard of incorruptibility, that it may come to the knowledge of a Judge that delay in the settlement of a case will be taken by the suitors in his Court to mean that he is waiting to be bribed; nay, that, pending the actual settlement, sums of money are actually being paid to the native subordinates of his Court, which are supposed to pass on to his hands.

But the influence of this same bureaucracy on actual evangelisation may not only be neutral but adverse. There are many instances on record of highly-placed English officials setting forward the cause of Missions by every legitimate means. But instances are not wanting of an attitude exactly the opposite. And in any case the indifference of Englishmen to the spiritual welfare of the country, as contrasted with their noble devotion to its moral and material interests, is the opposite of helpful to Missions. Such indifference it is easy to account for. To live among non-Christians, debarred by one's official position from attempting to draw them to Christ, is in itself to run grave risks of sinking down into total indifference not only about their spiritual welfare, but about the abstract truth or falsehood of the various religions they profess. The situation is so wholly anomalous that little, if any, blame can attach to individual officers. But the reader will readily see how disastrous may be its reaction on the attitude of Christians themselves. They are bound to treat other faiths with what tends to become contemptuous tolerance. And this leads to looking on one's own as but one among many attempts at the solution of that which is insoluble, as one of many approaches to an unknown and unknowable Being, if the sojourner in a heathen country has aught but the firmest of grips upon the faith in which he was trained. The influence, then, of English Society, and specially of English officialdom, while it makes in the highest degree for the moral elevation of India, cannot be regarded as favourable, can hardly be deemed as not adverse, to the Christianisation of the country.

I have indicated in these last sentences what weight should really be attached to the prejudice so terribly common among English residents in India, against active missionary efforts. The educational work of Missions, their ameliorating effect upon the people, on its social and moral side, elicits hearty sympathy from officials, both military and civil. But in the work of evangelisation they often refuse to believe, as being possible or even desirable. There is much to be said in their excuse. In the general estimate of results I shall have many failures to speak of. Among the earliest converts to Christianity there are many little better than runagates, many more whose spiritual force never rises to the normal level expected of followers of Christ.

The dropping of the shell of Caste, about which I have spoken above, has left them without the support which a traditional system afforded, unequipped with the spiritual armour which life requires for its defence when lived under "a law of liberty."

Then, one scandalous native Christian brings more discredit on the Gospel than can ever be visibly redeemed by the lives of twenty adherents who have never figured in the Law Courts, or been heard of beyond their own villages.

Of the total indifference of Europeans to the work

of Missions among the heathen the following may serve as an example. A lady travelling in the country was visiting a European family in the military cantonment of Poona. Being deeply interested in Missions, she made inquiries about the Anglican Mission in the native city close by, with a view to paying it a visit. Her hostess stoutly maintained that no such Mission existed, and the visitor left without seeing it. As a fact, the staff of that Mission, a mile and a half away, included four or five clergy, and fifteen or sixteen Sisters; its communicants were numbered by hundreds; it had six schools, of different grades, for Christian boys and girls, and its Church yields to none in the Diocese. But all this belonged to the native city, with its one hundred thousand inhabitants, a mile and a half away; while to the hostess, "Poona" was the cantonment, with its fashionable European Society, and "Christianity" meant parade service, as said on Sunday mornings.

In face of the many considerations which my readers have now had before them — Monism in Philosophy, Pantheism in Religion, Caste in Society, heredity and habit in the converts, secular education under Government, necessary neutrality in things official, indifference in Anglo-Indian Society — it cannot be matter for surprise if I say that wholesale conversions, indeed that rapid progress is not to be looked for at present in many parts of the country.

But let us see what progress there is,—quantitatively, for as much as this is worth, qualitatively, in so far as this is possible.

And even this, with a preliminary caution. Impatience for visible results is the "last infirmity" of enthusiasts—not for the unworthy reason that they wish to see something for their money, but as part of the very enthusiasm which makes them supporters of Missions. They must not make certain at present of rapid or striking advances. The mistakes of the Salvation Army, who have thought, in such a country as India, to swell the ranks of Christianity by the din of drums and trumpets, and by hysterical assurances of conversion, are only the extremest specimen of a totally false view of Missions. And within my personal experience, some earnest methodist missionaries have erred but little less seriously.

By one means, indeed, we might hope that results would be rapidly developed. Should God see fit, in His goodness, to raise up native evangelists, who shall be to the Gospel of His Son what many a Hindu reformer has been to revivals of heathenism, then districts and provinces might be won within the lifetime of the present generation. Such results can hardly be obtained by the work of any European. In the hands of Indian evangelists Christianity would adapt itself in detail to the country it was destined to win. The inexpressible touch of sympathy which countryman has with fellow-countryman, and Asiatic with Asiatic, would effect, under the guidance of the

Spirit, what we European Christians can never hope to approach. How soon God may will to do this, or how long He may delay its accomplishment, it is absolutely vain to speculate.

The advent of a great personality is one of the inexplicable mysteries which He hides within the counsels of His providence. We can pray for it, and in a sense we can hasten it. The patient underground work which Missions are doing in the present is at all events preparing the field, within which spiritual genius may—I will not say be expected to germinate, but—at least have room for growth, if it be planted by God's own hand. To work with imperturbable patience for results which may be centuries in coming is the task now laid upon Christendom. To promote such work among ourselves, by laying down principles for its accomplishment, is the aim of this little book. Results I can only handle in so far as they illustrate principles.

CHAPTER II

RESULTS FROM THE STATISTICAL POINT OF VIEW: QUANTITATIVE RESULTS.

I BEGIN, then, by quoting some figures. Counting heads can go for but little in such a calculation as this. Yet even as a matter of statistics the results are far from contemptible.

I offer no figures of my own, but shall lay before my readers statistics taken from the census of 1901, as compared with that of ten years earlier.

The gross population of the country showed an increase, in those ten years, of between seven and eight per cent. The increase in the number of Christians amounted to about thirty per cent; the totals being 2,037,055 in 1891, and 2,664,366 in 1901. That is to say, the increase of Christians was somewhere about four times as great as the natural growth of the population. For every hundred inhabitants in 1891, there were to be found about 107 in 1901. But for every hundred Christians in 1891, there were to be found about 130 in 1901.

The increase varied much in different parts of the

country. In Assam, it came to as much as 120 per cent; while in some other provinces or regions it was as low as twenty per cent. But the figures, taken as a whole, show that for every child baptized as the offspring of Christian parents, as many as three Hindus or Mahommedans or Aboriginals were received into the fold as converts.

The total increase of Christians in the ten years under review came to 627,759. The actual figures of the census, arranged under British Provinces and Native States, are as follows:—

PROVINCES

Madras	983,888
Bengal	224,717
Bombay[1]	171,214
Burma	129,237
United Provinces (N.-W. P.)	68,841
Punjab and Frontier	38,228
Assam	33,595
Central Provinces	17,791
Coorg	3,160
Ajmer-Merwara	2,362
Berar	1,748
Baluchistan	425
Andamans and Nicobars	135
	1,675,341

[1] Bombay includes 2,988 in Sindh, and 478 at Aden.

STATES AND AGENCIES

Travancore and Cochin	906,789
Mysore	39,585
Hyderabad	15,357
Bombay States	10,105
Baroda	7,543
Central Indian Agency	3,715
Bengal States	3,053
Rajputana	1,368
Central Provinces States	576
United Provinces States	447
Punjab States	285
Kashmir States	202
	989,025
Grand Total	2,664,366

These figures are reprinted from the *Church Missionary Intelligencer* for July, 1902.

Now in dealing with the figures above, one very encouraging fact must always be borne in mind—the extraordinary fewness of the workers as compared with the work to be overtaken; showing, as this does, how much more might be effected if their numbers rose to something more adequate. The total population of India in 1901 amounted to, roughly speaking, 294,000,000. The Mission-workers, male and female, clerical and lay, educational and strictly evangelistic, numbered 3415, not including Roman Catholic clergy, etc., such as are doing strictly missionary work.[1] India, then, we may consider, on a rough estimate, to contain about as many inhabitants as London multiplied by sixty-five. Now what would be said about the hopes of Christianity for even remaining stationary in London, if the total number of workers among all its many denominations bore the same proportion to its inhabitants as evangelistic workers in India bear to its teeming millions? Yet India has to be converted, not merely to be maintained in Christianity. And, crowded as India is, compare the extent of its surface with that of the British metropolis. London lies in four counties, and covers but a portion of these. India is as large as Europe, with the Russian Empire cut off.

It will be seen, then, that, even quantitatively regarded, the present results of Missions on the mass of Indian Society, while they cannot be called very large as compared with the total population, are per-

[1] By far the larger number of Roman Catholic clergy or religious are working exclusively among their own flocks. Of the remainder there are some who confessedly devote their time to proselytising from other Missions. "The heathen," one of them said to a well-known Anglican missionary, "may possibly be saved by the light of nature. Your people know too much for that: their only hope lies in being received into the Catholic Church." Dr. Meurin, the then Roman Catholic Bishop of Bombay, went among the native Christians of the S.P.G. Mission at Ahmednagar, while I was absent through illness, bribing unworthy native agents of ours to join him in a raid on our people, and merely telling ignorant converts, who knew no difference, that he was the Bishop of Bombay, by which they understood that it was their own Bishop who was visiting them.

ceptible, unchallengeable, nay, considerable. Father Benson, of the Cowley Society, in a paper published some years ago in the Indian *Church Quarterly Review*, made a careful historical comparison between the spread of Christianity in Europe in the early days of the Church and the progress now toward in India. The conclusion at which he arrived was that, taking them each as a whole, India was being christianised now, from a numerical point of view, more rapidly than Europe was then; and that, from the point of view of carefulness about baptizing, there was nothing in India to-day to be compared to the scandalous cases of so-called mass-conversions which disgraced Christianity in Europe in not a few periods then. This calculation was made before the results of the last census had thrown new light on the subject. He might have gone further than he did, had he had before him then the figures for 1901. For all his calculations were based on an increase of twenty-five per cent between 1881 and 1891; while the growth displayed by the last census amounted to thirty per cent.

CHAPTER III

RESULTS FROM THE MORAL POINT OF VIEW: QUALITATIVE RESULTS

BUT to pass to Qualitative Results. Any estimate formed about these must be, from the necessities of the case, rather matter of general impression, no matter how carefully corrected, than of actually verifiable fact. How rough and how fallible it must be, I desire to proclaim from the first. Father O'Neil of the Cowley Society was asked one day, in my hearing, what results had followed from a Mission which he had held in an English parish. "I will tell you at the Day of Judgment," was his characteristic reply. And such must, to some extent, be mine about results in the Mission Field in India.

Still, as far as can be told in this world, I am bound to attempt such an estimate. If my treatment of it appear somewhat desultory, it shall not be chargeable, if I can help it, with inaccuracy through sentiment or through prejudice.

But one preliminary consideration must first be placed before the reader; since alike the formation and the correction of any such general impressions are apt to be sadly vitiated by the attitude in which every Englishman must approach the life of Orientals.

First, the sins and faults and deficiencies to which Indians are specially liable are those which appear most odious in the eyes of Europeans and Englishmen. The ghastly untruthfulness of Hindus—the result of centuries of Caste, with all its demoralising conditions, and aggravated, as it certainly is, by the sad intellectual uncertainty which comes of a reasoned Pantheism—reduces the moral fibre to something most contemptible to us.

Then the mercenariness of the native character, with the marvellous pettiness of detail into which it is prone to descend, is almost incredible to Englishmen. It is partly, no doubt, to be accounted for by the abject poverty of the country. Experience of the poor among ourselves often opens the eyes of their helpers to the terrible temptations to mercenariness, and also to pecuniary dishonesty, which result from straitened means. But what would be poverty to an Englishman is wealth to the average Hindu.

Again, treachery, that resource of the slave, besets the Hindu character, and is regarded with an absence of reprobation, in ordinary native society, which staggers well-wishers of the country, to the total alienation of their sympathy.

When the remains of vices like these display themselves in converts to Christianity, the tendency of the English looker-on is to condemn all Missions wholesale for not having rooted them out, and that in the first generation, and by the bare fact of conversion. When a man has once faced the great ordeal, has sacrificed his caste and his all for the sake of becoming a Christian, it may seem perhaps at first sight as though everything must instantly give way before the depth and the power of his conversion; that he will become more thoroughly Christian than the man who has been trained from his youth in the doctrine and practice of the Gospel.

Now all preconceptions like these are falsified by actual experience. Among the crosses of the Christian Missionary, and the stumbling-blocks to the Christian looker-on, disillusion on this point stands first. The influences of heredity and of habit are not thus easily thrown off. Saintly converts, thank God! are to be found; respectable converts, by the thousand; alas! scandalous converts, not a few. But it constitutes an everyday experience that it is not in the first generation that the developed fruits of the Gospel begin, as a rule, to appear. Not the convert, baptized as an adult; and not the convert's children, brought up by half-trained parents; but the children's children of the converts, themselves baptized in childhood, and brought up in enlightened homes, display the fruits of the Gospel as we fondly expect to find them in those who accept it as converts. The failures and sins of the last-named are exactly what naturally follow as the fruits of an age-long heredity, and of early habit and training.

But after allowing for these considerations, there are two most important points which present themselves to every observer, comparing or contrasting Hindus with even Christians of the first generation. The terrible melancholy of Hinduism, the blank lack of interest in life which appear in the manner and the countenance, to indicate its prevailing temperament, disappear at once in the convert. The brightness and cheerfulness of the Gospel develop, especially in the young, quite a new capacity for enjoyment: the interest of life seems trebled.

Again, a sojourn in a Mission where the management of girls is understood, brings out a marvellous contrast between all that is visible there and the impression which comes irresistibly when a man brought up in England sees womanhood as found among Hindus.

The conception of modesty and purity which obtains among Hindu women is absolutely different in kind from what we expect among Christians. Not to look a man in the face, to look past him, to shun his eye, is the instinct of a Hindu woman who respects herself and her position. The frank, unconscious gaze which is taken as a matter of course in one's dealings with Christian women, the sense that there is nothing to avoid, the delicacy, which takes itself for granted, because it is incapable of evil, have become an inherited instinct in well-trained English girls. Now all these are so unintelligible in any but Christian society that the liberty accorded to women by the common usage of Europe appears to the Hindu mind as simply a courting of licence. The contrast in this respect between the native Christian girl and the other women of the country, untouched by Christian tradition, is something too palpable and unmistakable to be called a mere impression. To have seen it is to think of Christianity as introducing "a new Creation."

I must make, then, two marked exceptions when I speak of the prevailing low standard to be found among Indian converts in regard to many virtues associated with the Gospel of Christ. But before I leave this subject, I desire to suggest to the reader that when English and Indian Christians form estimates, each of the other, perhaps the sense of deficiency, of a standard not wholly adequate, may not be all on one side. If the faults of the Indian Christian are peculiarly odious to the Englishman, perhaps there are traits in ourselves which astonish our Indian brethren as wholly unaccountable in Christians.

The truth about impressions such as these is not easily arrived at, I must own. I have said, and that more than once, before English and Indian Christians, how much I should like to know how the natural pride of an Englishman—what we call our self-respect—really strikes a Hindu Christian, whose capacity for self-distrust has perhaps struck the Englishman as abject; or, again, how European luxury—or what must seem such to Hindus—impresses our native brethren, to whom ordinary tables and chairs appear to be quite a superfluity, and who can be fat and well-liking on a diet which to us would be starvation.

But enough of allowances and minimisings. There are saints among Hindu Christians.

Let me write, then, of one whom I knew—of the Brahmin Nilkant Goreh, baptized as Nehemiah. Long before I first went to India I was shown by a *quondam* missionary a photograph of a native in a cassock, with the words: "This is the most Christ-like man I know." After many opportunities of observation, and some approach to intimacy, I understood what the speaker meant. There were many of the weaknesses of the native—an extraordinary want of practicality about the smaller details of life; a preponderance of intellectual refinement, at the cost, to some extent, of the growth of the religious affections; phenomenally prolonged indecision, because every side of every question required to be endlessly studied before the mind could be made up. But there were found in this typical Brahmin not one of the Hindu vices set forth in what precedes.

There was an absolute loyalty and straightforwardness, a chivalrous superiority to mercenariness, a truthfulness, transparent and complete, which very few Englishmen could equal. In him, that first act of self-sacrifice did seem to have cut out by the roots the Hindu works of the flesh. To have known even one such man among one's native Christian friends, the whole number being so few, was to have lived down once and for ever any prejudice against Indian Missions. But although one knew only one Goreh, there were other Christians to be met, and that not very infrequently, of whom any Church might be proud.

In one respect, indeed, they stand far above most Englishmen—worship comes more spontaneously to them. The attitude of prone submission in the acknowledged presence of Deity, the act of sheer adoration, of exalting God as God, and assuming the attitude of a creature in the presence of the Infinite Creator, is to be seen in a native congregation far more frequently and far more deeply than in one composed of Europeans.

The weakest side, perhaps, of native Christian life is that which has already come out in my comments on Xavier and Schwartz, and the results which their Missions produced. The power of standing alone, not to say of spreading the Gospel, is sadly wanting among natives. Every candid English missionary must acknowledge that, for the present at least, the

Religion for which he has laboured remains an exotic in India. The descendants of Xavier's converts have held their own, it is true: they do nothing to set forward the Gospel. The children of Schwartz's converts, in the second or third generation—some of them, I fear, in the first—relapsed altogether into heathenism. And in every Mission in the country there is to be seen, in its most aggravated form, what Professor Drummond[1] described as "Parasitism in religion"—inability to stand alone, to live any life in Christ which is not dependent on others for maintaining its very existence.

Every Christian priest of strong character, in whatever country he works, must face the difficult problem of the scope and the proper limitations of personal influence over others—how far his own strength of character may prove the weak point in his work—how people, by clinging to him, may rise to a standard of observance which is wholly unnatural to them—how they may take his spiritual magnetism for a genuine work of the Holy Ghost, transforming their personal characters. The difficulty is there, and must be met. The point to be thought out and decided is, Where is he to draw the distinction? What discriminates personal influence as a means of drawing men to Christ from that same personal influence putting self instead of Christ? At what point must man stand aside, lest the shadow of

[1] In *Natural Law in the Spiritual World.*

his own personality come between the Redeemer and the redeemed?

But if every minister of Christ must sometimes be questioning himself thus, the missionary must be doing so constantly. Before he baptizes a convert, and after the baptism has taken place; when work has to be started in a neighbourhood; when a community, christianised, as it may seem, has to be raised to spiritual independence; when a candidate is accepted for Ordination, and when he is placed in sole charge, the question must again be raised—are we courting scandals and apostasies, or are we merely requiring of natives what Christianity entitles us to expect? An overwhelming proportion, I am persuaded, of the difficulties and the actual collapses of missionary work in India is due, not to conscious hypocrisy on the part of converts to Christianity, but to failure to ask these questions, or to decide on them with reasonable prudence.

To hold a nascent Church too long under foreign control were, of course, to do injustice to it and to the Grace which might support it. But to attempt to develop it prematurely were an evil indefinitely greater. Mistakes in both directions have been made, and are still being made. If missionaries of our Communion have been justly chargeable sometimes with fathering their converts too sedulously, the opposite, and more dangerous, error has characterised some Nonconformists; some excellent American

Independents having been the most prominent offenders.

If doctrinaire English Radicals, placed in high office in India, have made the mistakes that they have done in trying to force on the country some measures of local self-government for which it is totally unfit, and if their deluded promoters have not been convinced by results, it is scarcely perhaps to be wondered at that missionaries from the home of democracy have erred in a similar way. Undeniable it certainly is that the results, in American Missions, of leaving the native pastors to sink or swim alone have been disastrous to them and to their flocks.

The question has been raised among ourselves, how soon a native Episcopate may be formed, and may be left independent. That it should ever have been opened for discussion, as though it could be settled by ourselves, only indicates how impossible it is for the best and most earnest of men to understand the conditions of India without having lived among Indians. In the face of the conspicuous ability which has often been displayed in the country, when some tried native statesman has administered a kingdom alone, it would be mere presumption on our part to insinuate that a native priest might not be found to-morrow who would be fit to administer a Diocese. But considering how impossible it has proved to place even outlying Missions under the care of native priests without European supervision;

considering the fewness in all of the native Presbyterate in India; it is simply absurd for the present to speculate on the subject at all. When God raises up the man, the English Bishops in India will not be slow to discover him, and, having discovered him, to put him forward. Meantime, in the absence of such a personality, the abstract raising of the question seems to me to be totally futile.

My general conclusion about results—what they are, and how to obtain them—comes, then, to something like this—that there are as great variations among Christians in India as there are in England, and not, perhaps, very much greater. That the faults and the shortcomings to be found there are simply racial characteristics, not wholly redeemed by God's Grace.

CONCLUSION

CONDENSATION OF CONCLUSIONS ARRIVED AT

AND now I must offer, ere I close, a few definitely thought-out conclusions, as the result of all that has gone before.

This first, then—that the "Acts of Apostles" form a manual of missionary methods, divinely prepared for the Church, for her guidance "to the Consummation of the Age"—and that not only for instruction but for warning: that, studied as they ought to be studied, in the light of our modern experience, they will be found to have a bearing on work under all combinations of circumstances, and among all conditions of men. To this end, they must be fearlessly investigated; we must, without hesitation or scruple, pick out from their impartial record not only examples but warnings—must not take each act of each Apostle as necessarily a model to be followed, but must look at the consequences of each, as candidly given us by St. Luke, or to be gathered from the rest of the New Testament; that we must pronounce in the light of what followed that here did the enthusiasm of the Church, or here did the inexperience of St. Paul, lead to actions or omissions or procedure which issued in disaster or in failure; that the course which was blessed with good issues is not more divinely bequeathed to us for our guidance at the present day, than was the course which led to the opposite divinely recorded for our warning. And in each case, I am firmly persuaded, the consummate art of St. Luke, concealed under the graceful ease with which he groups his brilliant pictures, has selected typical instances by which to set before us to-day the stages in missionary evolution, through which the purposes of God were wrought out by human endeavour or hindered by human imperfection.

It were a task well worth fulfilling to follow this out in full detail. I can but indicate it here as a suggestion.

Next, I take it that the first of the lessons, which have partly been learnt from the past and have partly to be confirmed in the future, is that, for India, perhaps for most Mission fields, the primary, indispensable condition for escaping disaster or failure is the simple—but for manifold instances, I would say the surely obvious—principle that a man cannot work over a province, and yet prove as effective and successful as if he confined himself to a district. Painful years of correcting mistakes may be entailed on himself and his successors, if he, by neglecting this precaution, have committed himself and the Church to a task which is simply impracticable—that of keeping her infants in Christ full-nourished with their diet of milk, while they are treated, as regards opportunities, in a way which were trying and dangerous for souls full-grown in the faith.

This principle, obvious though it seems, has been as grossly violated or forgotten in some of our Missions to-day, as though neither a Xavier nor a Schwartz had nullified his glorious self-devotion by neglecting it centuries ago. And the consequences have been lamentable and hindering. Territorial limitation, it is true, will not render a Mission successful, apart from qualities of greatness in the characters of those who conduct it. But one thing may be safely laid down—that, be the qualities of the workers what they may, the plan of restricting their operations to ground which can be properly worked will secure that they at least get fair play—that their energies shall not be frittered, and the hearts of their successors broken, over a struggle with impracticable conditions.

Take, for instance, the missionary life of one who was afterwards a Bishop, and a Bishop of a heroic type, Richard Valpy French, "the seven-tongued man of Lahore," as he was called for his linguistic achievements. It is impossible to study it intelligently, with however sympathetic a mind, and to avoid the inevitable conclusion that much of his time and strength were simply wasted and lost over distant, sporadic expeditions in which no fruit could be reaped from all his unsparing devotion. The man was so original and so autonomous that perhaps it may be questioned, after all, whether he ever could have worked for a day along lines laid down by another. Yet plainly the lessons of the past were there, had he only traced them out—Carey and his ways, on the one hand, as the model, what to attempt, Schwartz and his ways, on the other, as the beacon, what to avoid, as regards concentration and diffusion. Yet we find this noble life losing half of its possible usefulness because it never was kept in the track by which chivalrous improvidence had been averted and solid economy brought about.

This first elementary concession to experience, nay, indeed, to common sense, ought to be rigidly enforced, I am persuaded, by the Bishop of every Diocese, the Committee of every Society, the head of every staff engaged in missionary work in India or anywhere else.

Then, this once granted and carried out, the question must everywhere arise, how best to bring to bear upon the work, how exactly to accommodate to one another, the two great leading principles by which each Mission must be guided within the territory actually occupied—the principle of concentration and the principle of diffusion, the method of consolidation and the method of wider extension. For each must play its part, though in ever-varying proportions, according to conditions and surroundings, in the development of a nascent Christianity. Is the Mission to be properly a Mission?—then even if its primary object be to work on concentrated lines, to consolidate an indigenous Church as the nucleus of future extension, it must still be considering from the first how many can be reached by the Good Tidings, how many can be brought into the Church with permanent benefit to themselves and with credit to the Gospel of Christ—it must remember the principle of diffusion. Is the Mission to be solid and successful? —then even though its primary object be at least to bring the sound of the Gospel to as many as will listen to its preachers, it must so carry out that object as to create from its earliest converts a veritable "people of possession"; it must secure that its local diffusion be not so imprudently guided as that those who are brought to the Saviour by profession and by Sacramental Initiation, should miss being nourished in the Faith by feeding on the milk of the word—it must remember the principle of Concentration.

How the two are to be proportioned to one another—at what point the intrepid pioneer must hold back from some tempting enterprise, lest he weaken his work at head-quarters, and substitute quantity for quality—where exactly the believer in quality must consider that work for the unconverted has a primary claim on his energies, so that ministry to his children in Christ must give way to it in certain points—about this it must be freely admitted that it will lie with every Diocesan, with every head of a great Mission to work out its proper salvation according as the Spirit shall guide him. What I plead for with earnest insistence is that it should not be left in each case for the authority immediately concerned to work out the problem afresh in forgetfulness of the lessons of the past, to settle it crudely and empirically by experiences of failure and mistake, as if all this had not been done by pioneers of centuries ago, to say nothing of more recent experimenters. It should no longer be possible, I maintain, for a Bishop, in taking over his Diocese, for the Head of a great Mission-staff on taking over his new position, to find that his time must be spent in overtaking, or trying to overtake, the results of his predecessor's mistakes; those mistakes being due, perhaps, to a single preventable cause, lack of systematised, chronicled experience handed on from generation to generation.. Let each new extended Mission, each old one, when it makes new departures, set out with principles before it, with experience recorded for its benefit:—here and here did one Mission fail, because it worked over too wide a field; here and here did another succeed, because it always bore this in mind—that to build up its converts in the faith was of indefinitely greater importance than to bring fresh neophytes in while the old were left unedified; at this point did progress become permanent, because the method of concentration was brought in to supplement and to stiffen diffusion; at that did over-concentration degenerate into hotbed unhealthiness, because opportunities of extension were not sought out and made use of.

Be experience brought to bear in these ways: be work undertaken from the first with these results of past labours kept steadily before the workers. Be principles thus laid down, to be applied at every turn to anticipate possible mistakes, and to correct them, if once they have been made, and before they are rendered irreparable—and Method, systematised working, will render much impossible which has marred the endeavours of the past, will add fresh fruitfulness and safety to all that enthusiasm can effect.

This applies to all Missions in all countries; though it has a very special application under the circumstances of Indian work, among people enfeebled by Caste.

Next, a point applying only to India—over which much controversy has been held, which will be hotly contested, as I know, by some excellent missionaries now—Caste, in its every manifestation, is to be treated from the first, in all Missions, as the deadly antagonist of the Gospel, with which league or truce is impossible. Root-and-branch extermination is the only measure to be dealt to it. In its essence, the outcome of Pantheism, nay, its necessary, inevitable expression, it contradicts the Gospel of Christ in principle as well as in detail. For, deliberately and under terrible sanctions, it adopts, and acts on the principle that the relations of man with man—worse still, of man with God—are based upon physical descent and not upon moral Redemption, still less upon spiritual character. It goes back to the identical standpoint from which man's relations with God were viewed by the Jewish people before it was proclaimed by the Baptist that it was vain to have Abraham to one's father, and to base one's acceptance with God on the ground of ancestral descent. "From the days of John the Baptist until now," our Lord proclaimed to the world, "the Kingdom of Heaven suffereth violence, and the violent take it by force." Caste makes of it a close corporation, a social and religious citadel, impregnable to all but the elect—elect by birth into the world, with no regeneration even possible, in the spiritual sense of the word. And this exclusion from the Kingdom of Heaven is but typified, externally expressed, by the rigid, impassable lines, demarcating the low-born pariah from the high-born member of a caste, marking off the next castes to each other by a no less sharp line of cleavage. To be spiritually and morally reborn, to obtain a new nature in Christ, is, to the Christian, the only salvation. And this from the

Caste point of view must be absolutely and ever impossible.

Again, our Lord did away once for all with the distinction between the neighbour, who has a claim on us, and the rest of the world, who have none. And, how sadly and how humiliatingly soever the Christian world as a whole comes short of our Lord's ideal, it is impossible — the more impossible in principle on account of the failure in practice — to make terms with a Social System (which, in truth, is a religious system), the basis and ground of whose practice depends on this abrogated distinction.

Nor must the Church draw back, or entertain the idea of a compromise, for any hindrance or difficulty which may grow out of this her refusal. Far indeed must she ever be from underrating the force of these difficulties. The System against which she has to war has dominated the nation for centuries, and that with a ruthless power unlike aught else that I know of. And, like every other system which has ever dominated men's lives, it has obtained its commanding position from a certain special adaptation to the character of the people whom it enslaves. If now, after centuries of rule, it has become the moulding power which kneads its passive votaries into one homogeneous mass, from which character is all but crushed out, it must originally have taken its form, and derived its gigantic force from a something congenial and connatural to the genius of the race which it oppresses.

Which last thought branches out in two directions. It indicates a native congeniality between the system and the character of its votaries. They began by being in some way its originators, and now they are its inevitable product. To disentangle them, then, from its grasp needs a social and spiritual revolution which cannot be approached without trembling. For, even granted the possibility of its fulfilment—of which no one could dream for a moment apart from supernatural assistance—there remain the gigantic problems which would instantly present themselves for settlement. Caste owes its hold over men's characters to virtues inherent in itself, and not to the concomitant evils which are all that we often discern in it. And the danger must therefore present itself, that, in rooting out the tares of its abuses, we should pull up the good grain with them.

Before all that is involved in this the Church must surely stand trembling, as the Prophet stood trembling before his Lord, when he received his earliest call. "Ah, Lord God," she will certainly say, "I cannot speak, for I am a child." She will certainly be told, as he was, "Say not, I am a child: for thou shalt go to all that I send thee, and whatsoever I command thee thou shalt speak." But she must hear, along with this commission, those other most exacting words :—"See, I have this day set thee over the nations and over the kingdoms, to root out, and to pull down, and to destroy, and to throw down and"—then, and not till then—"to build and to plant."

Every missionary who goes to the country has to face this tremendous task, with the bitter cross of disillusionment which, when faced, it must necessarily bring with it. The whole social system of the country, he then begins to see, must utterly pass and be destroyed, if Christianity become the dominant religion. And how the reconstruction will come about, this he is not permitted to see. Alike the possibility of the throwing down and the details of the building up seem totally, hopelessly beyond him. He thought to build and to plant. He finds that his present task will be largely casting down and plucking up. If he be not the vulgar enthusiast which popular imagination may paint him, with no deeper appreciation of the problems than can be gained at a missionary meeting, among people who have never had to face them, he will know all the weaknesses of his work, and the frequent disappointments which will attend it. And in the face of all this he must go on, with, "Woe is me if I preach not the Gospel."

Here I would not be misapprehended. There are missionaries at work in the field who maintain that social distinctions must exist in India, as in England,

and that Caste perpetuated among Christians represents nothing more than these. A grosser fallacy were impossible. The social distinctions of England have much to be said in their disfavour. But at any rate they can be got over; they do not last from generation to generation, irremovable, obligatory, everlasting. Again, our own social distinctions, whether based on position or education, or, least desirable of all, upon money are known to be things of this world, to count for nothing at all in the affairs of the Kingdom of Heaven, to be non-existent in the Eyes of the Almighty. What have such distinctions as these in common with the lines of demarcation which separate Brahmin and pariah? Above all, our social distinctions are matter of practical convenience, of conventional present arrangement: they have nothing to do with religion. Nor are they considered for a moment to abrogate the moral obligation of mutual assistance and sympathy between those whom they separate in society. To compare them with the absolute cleavage which renders it pollution and disgrace to eat with a man of low caste, which deprives a man's sons of their birthright if the mother be without the pale, is a mere abuse of language, a device for persuading oneself that a difficulty of gigantic dimensions need not be immediately faced.

When I maintain that Caste must go, that to make terms with it is to break once for all with the practical Gospel of Christ, I am not to be taken for a moment as intending that the educated Brahmin, with all his social refinement, is to be treated as a traitor to Christianity, if he determine to marry his children to no one whose social position would render their happiness impossible; nor even that schools in India are not to maintain the same character which we take for granted in England, as places where cleanly children, who come from decent homes, need not find themselves side by side with others whose presence will offend them.

But it cannot be put too clearly, and cannot be repeated too often, that Caste and mere social distinction are totally different things, as different as Religion and Convention.

Another conclusion which I would draw is that the strictly Educational Mission has had its day and done its work; that no Bishop and no society ought to encourage the formation of schools or colleges as the first and most important work for a Mission, or, with possible exceptions, for individual priests here and there.

I am not, of course, speaking now of educational work among Christians, but of secular colleges and schools for the training of Mahommedans or Hindus in preparation for degrees or professions.

And where such work is going on, and cannot for the present be dropped, the strictest care should be enforced that the minds of all the pupils, non-

Christian and Christian alike, may not be confused and demoralised by finding that the same lessons, nay, sometimes the very same devotions, are used for all the school. I have been asked to examine a class in the Gospel according to St. John, in which not a single pupil was a Christian, or had a thought of becoming one. To me, it seemed a sacrilege to attempt it, and I was unhesitatingly constrained to decline. There are schools where non-Christian children are taught to say the same prayers which the Christians daily use. Are they, unbaptized as they are, outside the Covenant of Grace, not even feeling their way to it, to be taught to approach the Father with the very same words on their lips which are said by the members of Christ who are sitting on the benches beside them? Are the Christians to find themselves treated as though they, with their stupendous responsibilities and their marvellous, tender privileges, were held no nearer to God than the worshippers of Krishna or Kali? Or are these poor exiles from the Kingdom to be shown that, in the eyes of their teachers, they are held to have nothing to surmount, no barrier or partition to break down, before they may call God their Father in just the same sense as their schoolfellows who know Him and worship Him as such?

I have been treated as a mere sentimentalist, as disregarding the command to evangelise, because I held that the Mysteries of the Faith were not to be thus profaned, that the minds of believers and unbelievers were not to be thus confused.

Let it be shown from the Acts of the Apostles that a single Christian teacher, in the earliest days of the Church, ever taught one heathen listener, or even a Jew by Religion, a single Mystery of the Gospel, that the message brought by the Apostles to the unconverted world was aught but the need of a Saviour, and the fact that God had provided one —and the charge of mutilating the Gospel in its first proclamation to the heathen will deservedly lie against me. Till this can be brought home, I must hold as a matter of principle that work on Apostolic Methods, in this most important respect, is what will give Apostolic results.

Last, the ultimate success or failure of all that can be done for Hindus must depend, more than anything else, on the discernment exercised by missionaries in guiding the lives of their people through obedience on to ultimate independence. Nowhere else perhaps as in India does so much inevitably depend on the delicacy of care and adjustment with which this process goes forward. Nowhere else have characters been so stunted, and initiative rendered so impossible as among the bondsmen of Caste. Independence is a vice, and initiative a crime in the eyes of the votary of the system. To be slavish is the first of his virtues; acquiescence, the last word of his morality. To "stand fast in the liberty wherewith

Christ has made us free," to rule and order one's life on the single principle of love—this, and nothing less than this, should each Christian, in his measure and degree, make the goal of his ultimate endeavours. How little we attain it ourselves, how rampant is the vice of mere parasitism, of acceptance of conventional standards, among Christians everywhere and always! Yet a mere reproduction of Caste, with Christian standards behind it, is not what we ought to acquiesce in for even our Indian brethren.

How to strike the mean in all this, how to aim at ultimate liberty, at the least, and the least destructive, cost of present and rampant licence, is the problem which must be worked out in the history of every Mission, of every community of Christians, throughout the Continent of India. May He Who alone can effect it work it out in His own due time, by the guidance of His own Holy Spirit.